FREEDOM *from* EVIL SPIRITS

First published in 2019 by

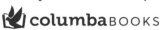 columbaBOOKS

23 Merrion Square North
Dublin 2, Ireland
www.columbabooks.com

Second Printing
ISBN: 978-178218-352-5

Set in Linux Libertine 10/14
Cover and book design by Alba Esteban | Columba Books
Cover illustration: The Temptation of St. Anthony by Martin
Schöngauer c. 1480-90. Engraving. The Metropolitan Museum of Art,
New York via Wikimedia Commons.
Illustrations pages 16, 72, 122, 200 and backcover by Louis Le Breton
from *Dictionnaire infernal* by Jacques Auguste Simon Collin de
Plancy, 6th edition, 1863 via Wikimedia Commons.
Printed by W&G Baird, North Ireland

FREEDOM

from

EVIL SPIRITS

RELEASED FROM FEAR, ADDICTION & THE DEVIL

PAT COLLINS C.M.

columba
BOOKS

"It is for freedom that Christ has set us free. Stand firm, then, and do not let yourselves be burdened again by a yoke of slavery."
(Gal 5:1)

In memory of the late
Sean O'Boyle
(1946-2017)

CONTENTS

FOREWORD

Expectations fill our hearts whenever Fr Pat Collins comes to speak at our conference in the Netherlands. Having a unique, classical way with words, he easily unites the different faith cultures and can bring his healing message of Jesus into the hearts of the assembly as well in this, his latest book.

Fr Pat has been talking about writing this book for a long time and I am pleasantly surprised to see its final publication. The title's mention of freedom is the state of being that most of us long for. To be free of the bondages that hold us back and suppress us from living in God's plan for our lives.

In his typical style, Fr Pat brings out a clear perspective and accentuates the urgent need in the Church for inner-healing and deliverance which frees us to hunger and long for a "true encounter with Jesus". An intimate relationship with our Lord, Saviour and Friend.

The availability of these pastoral resources, mentioned in this well-written book, summons us to not merely be freed from demonic influences, but also to be healed from psychological and physical illnesses. This can be realised through the gifts of the Holy Spirit operating, especially today, in the inner-healing and deliverance ministries in the Catholic Charismatic Renewal.

This book opens the door to help us see what exactly the enemy, his minions and human agents of darkness are hiding from us. Hosea 4:6 says it very clearly: "*My people are destroyed from lack of knowledge.*" We are in dire need of knowledge and the tools needed to 'break free' from being a slave to fear and stand on the victory already won by Christ and acknowledge our true identity as sons and daughters of the living God.

Thank you, Fr Pat for this stimulating pastoral work.

Ted M. Bauer
Co-founder of the Catholic Deliverance Ministry:
'House of Healing Den Bosch' in's-Hertogenbosch,
The Netherlands.

INTRODUCTION

The New Springtime Community in Dublin, to which I belong, is devoted to evangelising and training evangelisers. Like anyone committed to spreading the Good News, the members of our community focus on Christ's mission statement which he made public in the synagogue in Nazareth shortly after his baptism in the Jordan. On that momentous occasion he spoke these words: "The Spirit of the Lord is upon me, because he has anointed me to proclaim good news to the poor. He has sent me to proclaim *liberty* to the captives and recovery of sight to the blind, to set at *liberty* those who are oppressed, to proclaim the year of the Lord's favour" (Is 61:1-2). He then rolled up the scroll and gave it back to the attendant and sat down. The eyes of all in the synagogue were fixed on him and he said to them, "Today this Scripture has been fulfilled in your hearing."

Although it comes near the end of the quotation from Isaiah, the phrase, "to set at liberty those who are oppressed, to proclaim the year of the Lord's favour" is of central importance. In the Old Testament, as Leviticus chapter 25 indicates, there was a Jewish jubilee every 50 years. At that time, among other things, all slaves were set free. Jesus was declaring the advent of a spiritual form of liberation, when people would be set free from slavery to sin. As St Paul said in Rm 8:2, "the power of the life-giving Spirit has freed you from the power of sin". But Christ's proclamation of freedom had a wider relevance. In this book we will focus on three of the many other forms of liberty Christ brings "to those who are oppressed," namely, freedom from fear, addiction and the oppression of evil spirits whether over people or places. As St Paul said in Gal 5:1, "It is for freedom that Christ has set us free. Stand firm, then, and do not let yourselves be burdened again by a yoke of slavery."

It is my firm conviction that Christian freedom from all that binds and oppresses is an integral and indispensable aspect of the New Evangelisation called for by the Church. So this guide is a companion for my book, *Encountering Jesus: New Evangelisation in Practice*.[1] Although each of the four sections can stand alone in their own right, they are clearly interconnected because each one deals with an important aspect of Christian freedom. Not only that, they are all related, directly or indirectly with the activity of evil spirits. For example, although fear is a natural emotion, and addictions are forms of illness, nevertheless the devil can and does exploit them in order to lead people into sin and thereby to separate them from themselves, others and God. Speaking of fear, St Francis de Sales said in part 4, sec. 11 of his *Introduction to the Devout Life*, "With the single exception of sin, anxiety is the greatest evil that can happen to a soul." In like fashion, David Schoen, author of *War of the Gods in Addiction* says that addiction itself is a malevolent, murderous force, which is not amenable to reason or the treatments which can ameliorate other forms of mental illness. If unchecked, it can devour every aspect of the person's life and end in tragedy. This book does not pretend to be an exhaustive description of the different forms of Christian liberation or the many natural and supernatural ways of experiencing them. The different sections are written in a way that includes many headings, sections and subsections. Hopefully, this approach will contribute to both accessibility and clarity. It is also hoped that, despite their limited scope, these chapters will prove to be a helpful and practical resource. There are many excellent books available on all the topics covered, so a bibliography is included at the end of the volume.

This book is the result of what is referred to as theological reflection of a pastoral kind. Arguably there are two kinds of knowledge. Firstly, there is an academic, bookish kind and secondly, there is a practical, hands-on kind. It is sometimes referred to as praxis, i.e., the process of

---

1   (Luton: New Life, 2017).

using a thory or something that you have learned in a practical way. Pope Francis adverted to this distinction in pars. 231-232 of *The Joy of the Gospel* when he stated, "There exists a constant tension between ideas and realities. Realities simply are, whereas ideas are worked out. There has to be continuous dialogue between the two, lest ideas become detached from realities. It is dangerous to dwell in the realm of words alone... Ideas – conceptual elaborations – are at the service of communication, understanding, and praxis." What is needed is to synthetise ideas with experience. Authors Evelyn and James Whitehead suggested in their groundbreaking book *Method in Ministry*,[2] that theological reflection of a practical kind consists of dialogue between three interrelated constituents:

1. *Tradition*, i.e., information that we draw from Scripture, the Church's magisterium, liturgy, Church history etc.
2. *Lived Experience* of real-life situations such as the many things that constrain human freedom, such as fear, addiction and oppressive evil spirits.
3. *Cultural Information* which includes such things as philosophy, sociology, psychology and anthropology.

By and large that is the method I have tried to adopt in this book. It is my hope that as a result of reading it and putting some of its many recommendations into practice, you yourself, and anyone you seek to help, can end up experiencing greater inner emancipation, and being able to say in the words of Martin Luther King Jnr, "Free at last! Free at last! Thank God Almighty, we are free at last!"

I want to take this opportunity of dedicating this book to the memory of the late Sean O'Boyle of Columba Press. He was a gentleman and a scholar, who was both kind and encouraging to me over a period of a quarter of a century. May he rest in peace. I am also grateful to Ted Bauer, an American from California, who lives in Holland. He is not only a member of the House of Healing ministry team in Den Bosch, in the Southern Netherlands he is also a published author who has a produced a very helpful handbook entitled, *Deliverance*

---

2   (New York: Sheed & Ward, 1995).

Ministry (2017). I am grateful to him for writing the foreword to this book. Quotations from the Scriptures are mostly taken from the *English Standard Version* and the *New International Version* of the Bible.

A Writer's Prayer

"For every sentence, clause and word,
That's not inlaid with thee, my Lord,
Forgive me, God, and blot each line
Out of my book, that is not thine."

– ROBERT HERRICK, (1591-1674)

PART ONE:

FREEDOM FROM FEAR

CHAPTER ONE

INTRODUCTION

Like many others, I have had to contend with debilitating feelings of anxiety and fear throughout the course of my life. Like a pair of handcuffs, they have often held me captive. As a result, I have tended to stick to my comfort zones, avoided taking risks, and as a result have frequently failed to seize the day by courageously embracing opportunities and challenges that presented themselves. In retrospect I can see that crippling anxiety and fear often robbed my life of spontaneity and fulfilment. In this reflection I will look at both.

I think that we could all agree that reason and feeling play a vital role in the lives of human beings. Broadly speaking, reason is orientated to the comprehension of objective truths, whereas feelings are orientated to the comprehension of values. Rather than being evoked directly by reality our thoughts and feelings are responses to our perception of reality, influenced as it is by such things as personal memories, beliefs, attitudes and circumstances. As a result, different people can feel quite differently about the same realities. It can be noted in passing that psychologists differentiate between emotions and feelings. One can have an unconscious emotion, e.g. anger, which is repressed. While it can affect the body in a psychosomatic way, e.g. as high blood pressure, it may not express itself in a conscious way in the form of a feeling to do with a current or past experience, such as hurt or loss.

Over the centuries, thinkers have asked the question, what are the basic human emotions or feelings? Some maintain that there are nine. For instance, Aristotle wrote, "By passions I mean anger, fear, confidence, envy, joy, friendly feeling, hatred, longing, emulation, pity and in general the feelings that are accompanied by pleasure and pain."[3] Some modern psychologists maintain that there are six basic human emotions or feelings; happiness, sadness, fear, anger, surprise and disgust. Recent studies in Glasgow University indicate that there are only four foundational emotions or feelings, namely, fear, surprise, anger and disgust. Be that as it may, it is significant that fear is mentioned in all three lists. Over the years when I have asked myself the question, what is the basic human emotion or feeling? I have come to the conclusion that it is fear.

ANXIOUS FEAR AS THE BASIC HUMAN EMOTION/FEELING

Philosophers rightly say that human beings are contingent creatures. In other words, as created beings we are not the adequate explanation of our own existence which is constantly under threat. There is an Irish proverb which encapsulates that notion when it says that, "life is a sigh between two mysteries". From a human point of view our brief time on earth seems to be preceded and succeeded by non-existence. This truth was illustrated by an oriental story about a man who was being chased by a fierce tiger. He escaped by climbing down the inside wall of a well. However, at the bottom he saw the gaping jaws of a big poisonous snake. Because he couldn't go up or down the unfortunate man had to cling on to a small bush which was growing from the wall of the well. As his strength began to fail him, he noticed that two mice, one black the other white, were nibbling away at the roots of the bush. Before long he would tumble to his death. But just then he noticed that there were two drops of honey on one of the bush's leaves. He licked the nectar. It tasted sweet as he waited for the end. Life is much the same. It is sandwiched between the nothingness that preceded our birth and which will follow our death when we will fall into "the wide womb of uncreated night".[4] If there are moments of sweetness in life, their ultimate meaning is called into question by the impending annihilation of death.

The Greek philosopher Epicurus put it this way: "I was not; I

---

3   *Great Treasury of Western Thought* (New York: Bowker, 1977), 258.
4   John Milton, *Paradise Lost*, Book 2, line 150.

became; I have been; I am no longer; that is all."[5] So our human existence, is constantly threatened by the inevitability of non-existence.
As Shakespeare reminded us in Act III, scene II of *Hamlet*, we are constantly in danger from "the slings and arrows of outrageous fortune,"
in the form of such things as unexpected accidents, illnesses, and
disasters. That awareness of objective mortality and danger evokes
the subjective emotion or feeling of anxious fear. So, I suspect that
anxious fear is the primordial human emotion or feeling.

It is worth noting that although anxiety and fear are closely related, they differ from one another. According to *Chambers Dictionary of
Etymology*, the English word anxiety is derived from the Latin *ange-
re*, "to choke or cause distress". Anxiety, therefore is a response to a
sense of generalised threat which usually has no particular focus. It is
evoked by everything in general and nothing in particular. The word
fear is derived from the Old English *faer*, which referred to uneasiness which is evoked by the perception of particular dangers whether
real or imaginary.

---

5   Quoted by Ceslaus Spicq, O.P, in *St Paul & Christian Living* (Dublin: Gill,
     & Son, 1964), 13.

CHAPTER TWO

EXISTENTIAL FORMS OF ANXIOUS FEAR

When I was a young man in my twenties, I read a book by Paul Tillich entitled *The Courage to Be*.[6] Its masterly treatment of anxiety and fear made a deep and lasting impression on me. In one particular section, Tillich suggested that existential, as opposed to neurotic anxiety, is normal and understandable as a response to the awareness of the contingency of everything that exists, including oneself. It is evoked by the threat of non-being and can be experienced in three principal ways.

Firstly, there is the fear of fate and death. It was a primary characteristic of the classical, Greco-Roman period.

Secondly, there is the fear of guilt, judgement and condemnation. It seemed to predominate in the era of the Protestant Reformation.

Thirdly, there is the fear of emptiness and meaninglessness. It seems to be the underlying mood in our relativistic, post-modern, post-truth society. It is evident in contemporary painting, music, literature, movies, theatre, philosophy etc. While each age may experience existential anxiety through a particular cultural lens, the other related forms will also be present in the background. We will look briefly at each of them.

A] *FEAR OF FATE AND DEATH*

Since the dawn of human self-awareness people have been afraid of the vagaries of fate and the inevitability of their own personal deaths and the deaths of the people they love. I was reminded of this when my late mother and I visited the ruins of Pompeii, a town in Southern Italy, which had been destroyed in 79AD by the volcanic eruption of Mount Vesuvius. As we walked the ancient streets, stood in painted villas, admired statues, and explored temples, theatres, and public buildings, we were constantly reminded of the inexorability of death.

6   (London: Fontana, 1962).

This was particularly obvious when we strolled down a street with tombs and sepulchres on either side. The inscriptions on the grave-stones and monuments, like so many of the classical period, bore witness to an anxious preoccupation with mortality. Contemporary Roman and Greek authors gave expression to that preoccupation. For instance, Greek writer Pindar (522-443BC) sadly mused, "O my soul, do not aspire to immortality, but exhaust the realm of the possible." Roman writer Lucretius (99-55BC) came to a similar conclusion when he wrote: "Everything is slowly dying and is moving towards the grave, worn out by the length of life's path."

Not surprisingly, in modern secular culture, where faith in God and an afterlife are declining, many people have a strong fear of their personal death. In his book, *The Denial of Death*, Ernest Becker argued that human civilization is ultimately an elaborate, symbolic defence mechanism against the awareness of mortality.[7] There was a very amusing scene in the movie *Moonstruck* which illustrated this point. Mrs Castorini, played by actress Olympia Dukakis, asked Johnny Cammareri why men need more than one woman, because she had discovered that her husband was having an affair with a younger female. Johnny explained, "When God made woman, he took a rib from Adam and made Eve. That left a big hole where that rib was, and man can never feel complete until he gets it back." Mrs Castorini went on to ask, "Why then, would a man need more than one woman?" His response was, "I don't know. Maybe it's because he fears death." She retorted, "That's it? Thank you for answering my question!" Like men who cheat on their partners and wives, usually with a younger woman, people have many ways of avoid-ing the subject of ageing and death, such as cosmetic surgery, hy-pochondria, avoiding the writing of a will, acquiring property and wealth, etc.

Not only is there a fear of personal death, nowadays there is also a fear of collective mortality as a result of the power of atom-ic weapons and the possibility of nuclear war. Many years ago,

7   (New York: Free Press, 1973).

Arthur Koestler said in a chapter entitled, "The New Calendar," in his book *Janus: A Summing Up*[8] that if he were asked to name the most important date in human history he would respond without hesitation by saying that it was August 6th 1945. He went on to explain that from the dawn of humanity until that fateful day, near the end of Word War II, every man, woman and child had to face the inevitability of his or her personal death as an individual. But, ever since the destruction of Hiroshima, mankind as a whole has had to live with the fearful possibility of its extinction as a species. So, Koestler proposed a revision of the normal dating method. He said that we should replace BC and AD by referring to BH, that is Before Hiroshima, and AH, After Hiroshima. In another book entitled, *How Long will the Human Species Survive on Earth?*, author David Grinspoon has said that besides the threat of nuclear war, human survival is also threatened by a number of other factors such as world population growth; human-induced global warming; killer asteroids and comets; and eventually a much hotter sun. I get the impression that younger people are especially fearful of these possibilities, and their fears are often mirrored in a succession of disaster movies.

B] *FEAR OF GUILT AND CONDEMNATION*

Existential anxiety can also find expression in feelings of guilt and condemnation. The experience of being judged and condemned by our own conscience leads to feelings of guilt whereas the fear of being judged and condemned by others leads to feelings of shame. The case of the woman caught in the act of adultery and dragged into the temple as a public sinner probably illustrated an understandable apprehension that was rooted in feelings of both guilt and shame (cf. Jn 8:1-11). Although the crowd judged and condemned the woman in the light of Lev 20:10, Jesus refused to do so in a way that not only assuaged her fear, it also absolved her from her sense of shame and guilt. The fear of losing self-acceptance and the acceptance of

8   (London: Picador, 1983).

others is a large and important subject. It will not be dealt with here, but there are useful books available on the matter.[9]

Instead we will focus on one particular aspect, namely the fear religious believers can have of being judged and condemned by God, who is just and gives to each person what his or her behaviour deserves. This could mean that because of grievous sins the person might be afraid of eternal separation from the divine presence and love. That is a horrifying prospect. It is said that Augustinian monk, Martin Luther (1483-1546), was so terrified of this possibility that sometimes he used to writhe in anguish upon the ground, crying, "How can I obtain a God of grace?" He only experienced relief when he came to believe that he would be put at rights with God solely by his faith in Christ rather than by any merit or good work of his own. As Luther testified, "here I felt that I was altogether born again and had entered paradise itself through open gates."

St Ignatius of Loyola (1491-1556) suffered from severe scrupulosity. In his *Autobiography* he told us in the third person that, "although he realised that those scruples did him much harm and that it would be wise to be rid of them, he could not do that himself". Indeed, he admitted that they tormented him so much that he had been tempted to commit suicide. But realising, he said, "that it was a sin to kill oneself", he shouted, "Lord I will do nothing to offend you". He testified that his morbid preoccupation with guilt and condemnation had been prompted by the evil spirit rather than the Spirit of God. In chapter three of his *Autobiography* he said, "I decided very clearly, therefore, not to confess anything from the past any more; from that day forward I remained free of those scruples and held it for certain that Our Lord through his mercy had wished to deliver him."[10]

Not so many years later, St Francis de Sales (1567-1622) was

---

9   Daniel Green Ph.D. and Mel Lawrenz Ph.D. *Overcoming Guilt and Shame* (Waukesha, WI: WordWay, 2014).

10   *The Autobiography of St Ignatius of Loyola with Related Documents*, ed. John C. Olin (New York: Fordham University Press, 1992), 36.

assaulted by a similar fear of final condemnation. While a student in Paris he had been upset by the Catholic rather than the Calvinist doctrine of predestination. The spectre of possible separation, for all eternity, from the God he loved, caused him acute anxiety for a number of months. He resolved his problem in a curious and revealing way. He reckoned that if he was predestined to enjoy the presence of God, so be it. If he was to be denied that great joy, so be it. In the meantime, he had the opportunity to love God with all his strength. As author Wendy Wright has observed in her book *Bond of Perfection: Jeanne De Chantal And Francois De Sales,* "He was free, not in knowing, but free to love. All the rest was unimportant, for what was most essential for him was the pure love of God."[11] In other words, Francis overcame his anxiety by willing to love God in an unconditional way that did not depend on either the prospect of punishment or of reward.

In the course of my pastoral work over the years I have met with many people who were anxious, not so much about the prospect of impending death, as the likelihood of having to face God as a demanding judge in the particular and general judgments. As St Paul said in Rom 2:5-6, "because of your stubbornness and your unrepentant heart, you are storing up wrath against yourself for the day of God's wrath, when his righteous judgment will be revealed. God will give to each person according to what he has done." Not surprisingly, some people are really afraid, not without reason, that because of their many failures and omissions, they might be on the wide road that leads to destruction which, as Jesus warned, many people take (cf. Mt 7:13-14).

C] THE FEAR OF EMPTINESS AND MEANINGLESSNESS

During the 20th Century prominent psychologists gave different answers to the question, what is the deepest need of human beings?

- William James (1842-1910), an American psychologist, said: "The deepest principle of human nature is a craving to be appreciated."

---

11   (New Jersey: Paulist Press, 1985), 59.

- Sigmund Freud (1856-1939) said that the deepest human need was for love, pleasure and satisfying work.
- Alfred Adler (1870-1936) suggested that the fundamental human need was a desire for power as an antidote to low self-esteem.
- Carl Jung (1875-1961) was of the opinion that what people wanted most was individuation and wholeness of personality.
- Abraham Maslow (1908-1970) maintained that the fundamental need was for self-actualisation as a result of peak experiences of a transcendent kind.
- Viktor Frankl (1905-1997) proposed another foundational desire. He said that the fundamental human need was a sense of unconditional meaning.

While there is some truth in each of these points of view, I am inclined to agree with Frankl. But therein lies a problem because modern culture believes that there is neither an ultimate purpose nor meaning to human life. For example, modern evolutionary theory maintains that, rather than adapting to changing environmental conditions as French scientist Jean-Baptiste Lamarck (1744-1829) proposed, evolution is the result of blind, random mutations. For example, Neo-Darwinist, Richard Dawkins wrote in his book *River Out of Eden*, "In a universe of blind physical forces and genetic replication some people are going to get hurt, other people are going to get lucky, and you won't find any rhyme or reason in it, nor any justice. The universe we observe has precisely the properties we should expect if there is, at bottom, no design, no purpose, no evil and no good, nothing but blind, pitiless indifference."[12] Another scientist Christopher Potter concluded his bestselling book, *You Are Here: A Portable History of the Universe* with these words which are full of hopelessness, "In a modern world obsessed with certainty and things eternal, we might learn to live in the uncertainty of an unending scientific process. We want to believe that things last forev-

---

12   (New York: Basic Books, 1995), 133.

er, whether it is love, God or the laws of nature. . . Perhaps the best we can hope for is to live in uncertainty as long as we can bear it."[13]

It is said that we are living in a post-modern, relativistic age. Postmodernism maintains that, rather than being an objective fact, truth is an agreed upon fiction.[14] Nothing is absolutely certain, there is only an endless sequence of contexts and interpretations. At best, all we can know are partial, provisional truths. Postmodernism is also sceptical about traditional forms of knowledge. It subjects them to the hermeneutic of suspicion, by critiquing their presuppositions in a radical, deconstructing way. Commenting on contemporary culture Pope John Paul II, rightly observed in par. 91 of his encyclical *Faith and Reason*, "the time of certainties is irrevocably past, and the human being must now learn to live in a horizon of total absence of meaning, where everything is provisional and ephemeral. In their destructive critiques of every certitude, several authors have failed to make crucial distinctions and have called into question the certitudes of faith."

The diaries of Leo Tolstoy (1818-1910) illustrated that point by indicating that the great Russian novelist had a characteristically modern fear that life was ultimately empty and meaningless. When he reached 50, he had every reason to feel content. He had a loving wife and children, was wealthy, in good health, a successful writer, owned a 1,350-acre estate and as many as 300 horses. And nevertheless, he was unhappy. He felt that everything he possessed, and everything he had achieved was pointless. He wrote in his diary, "You can't close your eyes in order not to see that there is nothing ahead but the lie of freedom and happiness, nothing but suffering, real death and complete annihilation."[15] He was scared by death, not so much because it marked the end of his life, but because it robbed his life of any meaning it might appear to have.

---

13   (London: Windmill Books, 2010), 274.

14   Cf. Pat Collins CM, "Postmodernism and Religion" in *Doctrine & Life* (Jan 1999): 22-31.

15   Henri Troyat, *Tolstoy* (London: Pelican, 1970), 520.

Implicitly, the question he asked was not, "Is there life after death?" but rather, "Is there meaningful life before death?"

Henri Troyat says in his wonderful biography, *Tolstoy*, that the Russian novelist revealed in his diary that during his time of feeling empty and anxious, "he thought that he heard a sort of distant laughter. Someone was making fun of him, someone who had worked everything out beforehand long ago... 'I stood there like an idiot, realising at last that there was nothing, and never would be anything in life. And he thinks it is funny!'"[16] He was so oppressed by thoughts like these that he was tempted to commit suicide. Infact, he stopped taking his gun with him when he went out to hunt, so that, as he said himself, "I could not yield to the desire to do away with myself too easily." Tolstoy only overcame his feelings of despair when he recovered his childhood faith in God.

It is striking how St Therese of Lisieux (1873-1897) had a very similar experience. She said in her *Autobiography*, that she used to hear a mocking voice saying to her, "It is all a dream, this talk of a heavenly country, bathed in light, scented with delicious perfumes, and of a God who made it all, who is to be your possession in eternity!... All right, all right, go on longing for death! But death will make nonsense of your hopes; it will only mean a darker night than ever, the night of mere non-existence and annihilation."[17] During this dark night of the soul, Sister St Augustine reported: "Therese admitted something to me which surprised and confused me. She said, "If only you knew the darkness into which I've been flung! I don't believe in eternal life; I think, after this life there will be nothing more. Everything has vanished for me." But she added afterwards - and this is significant, *"All I have left is love."*[18] She believed in love. Implicit in that belief was a belief in God, who as 1 Jn 4:8 assures us, "is love". When I read Therese's poignant words I was reminded of something

---

16   Ibid., 520-4.
17   (London: Harvill Press, 1958), 255-256.
18   *St Therese of Lisieux by Those Who Knew Her*, ed. Christopher O'Mahoney (Dublin: Veritas, 1975), 195.

that Carl Jung said in his, *Memories, Dreams, Reflections:* "Man can try to name love, showering upon it all the names at his command, and still he will involve himself in endless self-deceptions. If he possesses a grain of wisdom, he will lay down his arms and name the unknown by the more unknown... by the name of God."[19]

CONCLUSION

Leo Tolstoy and Therese Martin gave voice to what has become a widespread fear in our post-truth society where there is a diminishing sense of ultimate meaning. Writing in par. 7 of *The Church in Europe* (2003), Pope John Paul II said, "The age we are living in, with its own particular challenges, can seem to be a time of bewilderment. Many men and women seem disoriented, uncertain, without hope, and not a few Christians share these feelings." In par 9, the Pope added, "It is therefore no wonder that in this context a vast field has opened for the unrestrained development of nihilism in philosophy, of relativism in values and morality, and of pragmatism – and even a cynical hedonism – in daily life." In par 10, the Holy Father concluded, "man cannot live without hope: life would become meaningless and unbearable without it." Arguably this is already the case for many people who live, as David Thoreau observed, "lives of quiet desperation".[20] That would help to explain why there has been such an increase in substance and behavioural addictions and why so many people suffer from mental health issues and commit suicide. They are so many ways of either deadening or escaping from their inner sense of pain.

---

19 (New York: Vintage, 1965), 354.

20 Chapter one, "Economy" in *Walden* (New Jersey: Princeton University Press, 2004).

CHAPTER THREE

OVERCOMING EXISTENTIAL ANXIETY

Over the years I have come to recognise that rather than being an enemy, existential anxiety can be the birthplace of true religion. As a creature I have come to experience, in the words of Friedrich Schleiermacher (1768-1834), a "feeling of absolute dependence"[21] and "a desire for the infinite"[22] which can only be satisfied by means of a personal relationship with God. This is a very evangelical notion. In his Beatitudes, Jesus declared, "Blessed are the poor in spirit, for theirs is the kingdom of heaven" (Mt 5:3). In other words, blessed are those who, for one reason or another, are aware of their radical need of God because it will lead them to experience right relationship with the Lord together with joy and peace in the Holy Spirit (cf. Deut 4:29; Rm 14:17). When the acknowledgement of fundamental human need is satisfied through a spiritual awakening and a transforming religious experience as a result of the outpouring of the Holy Spirit in and through the person of Jesus Christ, existential anxiety gives way to the joy of ultimate belonging as the basic or foundational human feeling. This, I think, is a point of fundamental importance and the most effective antidote to all kinds of anxiety and fear whether existential, neurotic or realistic.

St Bede tells a charming story in his *Ecclesiastical History of the English People* which illustrates this point. Pagan King Edwin of Northumberland allowed Bishop Paulinus to preach to him and some of his subjects including the pagan high priest, Coifi. When the king heard what Paulinus had to say, he asked the high priest for his reaction. Bede recorded what happened. "Coifi, immediately replied, 'in truth I declare to you that the religion which we have hitherto

---

21   *The Christian Faith* (London: T & T Clark, 2004), 12ff.
22   Pope Francis, par. 165 *The Joy of the Gospel.*

professed has, as far as I can learn, no virtue in it. For none of you has applied himself more diligently to the worship of our gods than I; and yet there are many who receive greater favours from you, and are more preferred than I, and who are more prosperous in all their undertakings. Now if the gods were good for anything, they would rather bless me, who have been more careful to serve them. It follows, therefore, that if upon examination you find those new doctrines which are now preached to us are better and more efficacious, we should immediately accept them without any delay'."[23]

Another of the king's chief men, approving of Coifi's words and exhortations, added: "The present life of man, O king, seems to me, in comparison with that time which is unknown to us, like to the swift flight of a sparrow through the room wherein you sit at supper in winter amid your officers and ministers, with a good fire in the midst, whilst the storms of rain and snow prevail abroad; the sparrow, I say, flying in at one door and immediately out at another, whilst he is within, is safe from the wintry storm; but after a short space of time he immediately vanishes out of your sight into the dark winter from which he has emerged. So this life of man appears for a short space, but of what went before or what is to follow we are utterly ignorant. If, therefore, this new doctrine contains something more certain, it seems justly to deserve to be followed." The other elders, and king's counsellors, by divine inspiration, spoke to the same effect. As a result, King Edwin received Christian baptism, and presumably his fears were reduced.

Not surprisingly, many non-believers in contemporary society have little or no conscious experience of the presence and merciful-love of God. It is surprising, however, that many church goers are also starved of genuine religious experience. In the 1950s, American psychologist Gordon Alport made a useful distinction in his book *The Person in Psychology: Selected Essays* which explained this anomaly. At first, he distinguished between "institutionalised" and

---

23   (London: Penguin Books, 1990), 130.

"interiorised" religion.[24] Later he talked about people with extrinsic and intrinsic religion.

- Allport defined *extrinsic religion* as religious self-centredness. Such a person goes to church as a means to an end - for what they can get out of it. They might go to be seen, because it is the social norm in their society, conferring respectability or social advancement. Going to church becomes a social convention.

- Allport thought that *intrinsic religion* was different. He described people who were intrinsically religious, as those who see their religion as an end in itself. They tend to be more deeply committed; religion becomes the organising principle of their lives, a central and personal experience.

Research indicates that generally those with intrinsic religiosity experience lower levels of anxiety and stress, freedom from guilt, better adjustment in society and less depression. On the other hand, those with extrinsic religion seem to experience increased levels of guilt, worry and anxiety. It is worth noting that psychologist Daniel Batson argued, that besides seeing religion as a *means* and religion as an *end* as Allport had done, there is also religion as a *quest*. He referred to the spiritual pilgrims of our time, who have neither extrinsic nor intrinsic religion as "Questers", people who see questions, and not answers, as being central to their religious experience. It is probable that religion as a quest is rooted in an unresolved feeling of anxious "creature feeling".[25]

I think that Aldous Huxley was correct when, speaking about fear and anxiety in his book *The Perennial Philosophy*, he wrote, "Fear, worry, anxiety – these form the central core of individualised selfhood. Fear cannot be got rid of by personal effort, but only by the ego's absorption in a cause greater than its own interests. Absorption

---

24   (Boston: Beacon Press, 1968).
25   A phrase used by Rudolf Otto in his book, *The Idea of the Holy* (Oxford: Oxford University Press, 1958), 10.

in any cause will rid the mind of some of its fears; but only absorption in the loving and knowing of the divine Ground can rid it of all fear."[26] For a Christian, the Divine ground Huxley referred to is God who is revealed as a result of a Spirit enabled union with his Son, who is our only way to the Creator. It could be said, therefore, that the levels of anxious fear in a Christian's life are a litmus test which measure the depth of his or her relationship with the Blessed Trinity. The more Christians are in communion with God, the more they will experience three simultaneous and interrelated joys; the joy of belonging to God, one's deepest self; and to the world of people and creation. As Pope Paul VI said in par. 1 of his Apostolic Exhortation on *Christian Joy,* "man experiences joy when he finds himself in harmony with nature, and especially in the encounter, sharing and communion with other people. All the more does he know spiritual joy or happiness when his spirit enters into possession of God, known and loved as the supreme and immutable good." When this is the case, a person is aware of the joy of ultimate belonging. It is the number one antidote to the three forms of anxious fear mentioned above.

Here is a striking example of what can be involved. Blaise Paschal was a child prodigy and a brilliant mathematician. When he reached the age of 30 he was a nominal Catholic and unmarried. His parents had died and his two sisters were preoccupied with their own lives. In other words, he was alone and inwardly needy. In Batson's terms he was a quester. The following year Blaise had a profound religious experience. Afterwards he wrote a description, of what had happened, on a piece of parchment which he sewed into his coat where it was found after his death. It said, "The year of grace 1654, Monday, November 23, day of Saint Clement, pope and martyr, and others in the martyrology. Vigil of Saint Chrysogonus, martyr, and others. From about ten-thirty in the evening to about half an hour after midnight. Fire. God of Abraham, God of Isaac, God of Jacob, not of the philosophers and savants. Certitude, certitude; feeling, joy, peace. God of Jesus Christ. "Thy God shall be my God." Forgetting the world and

---

26   (London: Fontana, 1966), 172.

everything, except God. He is only found by the paths taught in the Gospel. Grandeur of the human soul. "Just Father, the world has not known you, but I have known you." Joy, joy, joy, tears of joy... Total submission to Jesus Christ... Everlasting joy in return for one day's effort on earth."[27] That experience enabled Paschal to move from existential fear to the joy of ultimate belonging.

---

27   *Memorial.* http://www.users.csbsju.edu/~eknuth/pascal.html

CHAPTER FOUR

THREE ANTIDOTES FOR ANXIETY & FEAR

In science, an antidote is a remedy which counteracts the effects of a poison or toxin. Not only can it be administered in different ways, it can neutralise the poison or toxin in different ways also. For example, if a person was bitten by a poisonous snake, snake venom antiserum can be administered by means of injection. In this chapter we will look at psycho-spiritual antidotes to different forms of toxic fear.

A] *THE ANTIDOTE TO THE FEAR OF FATE AND DEATH*

Once a Christian passes from knowing about the person of Jesus to knowing him in person, he or she develops a sure faith in his resurrection from the dead. As Paul said in 1 Thess 4:13-14, "But we do not want you to be uninformed, brethren, about those who are asleep, so that you will not grieve as do the rest who have no hope. For if we believe that Jesus died and rose again, even so God will bring with Him those who have fallen asleep in Jesus." In 1 Cor 15:51-53 Paul added, "Behold, I tell you a mystery; we will not all sleep, but we will all be changed, in a moment, in the twinkling of an eye, at the last trumpet; for the trumpet will sound, and the dead will be raised imperishable, and we will be changed. For this perishable must put on the imperishable, and this mortal must put on immortality." Not surprisingly therefore, the preface of the Mass of the dead says, "In Him, who rose from the dead, our hope of resurrection dawned. The sadness of death gives way to the bright promise of immortality. Lord, for Your faithful people life is changed, not ended. When the body of our earthly dwelling lies in death we gain an everlasting dwelling place in heaven."

In Wis 1:13-14 we read, "God did not make death, nor does he rejoice in the destruction of the living." However, in Wis 2:24 we are told that, "by the envy of the devil, death came into the world." That is depicted in Gen 3:19 where the sin of Adam and Eve resulted in their having to endure death, "By the sweat of your brow you shall eat bread, Until you return to the ground, from which you were taken; For you are dust, and to dust you shall return." However, Jesus came not only to defeat the devil, but also to save us from sin and death by means of his sinless life and his saving death and resurrection. As Heb 2:14-15 says, "Since the children have flesh and blood, he too shared in their humanity so that by his death he might break the power of him who holds the power of death - that is, the devil - and free those who all their lives were held in slavery by their fear of death." Commenting on these verses, the New Testament volume of the *Expositor's Bible Commentary*, eds. Barker & Kohlenberger, says, "The defeat of the devil means the setting free of those he had held sway over who had been gripped by the fear of death. Fear is an inhibiting and enslaving thing; and when people are gripped by this ultimate fear - the fear of death - they are in cruel bondage. In the first century this was very real. The philosophers urged people to be calm in the face of death, and some of them managed to face their demise with equanimity. But to most people this brought no relief. One of the many wonderful things about the Christian Gospel is that it delivers men and women from the fear of death. They are saved with a sure hope of life eternal. A life whose best lies beyond the grave."[28]

St Therese of Lisieux witnessed to this truth when she said to one of her fellow Carmelites, "I cannot understand why people get so upset when they see their sisters die; we are all going to heaven and we will meet one another there again."[29] She would have rejoiced when reading these words in Rev 1:17-18, "When I saw him, I fell at his feet as though dead. But he laid his right hand on me, saying, "Fear not, I am the first and the last, and the living one. I died, and behold I am alive forevermore, and I have the keys of Death and Hades."

Those who, like St Therese, have intrinsic religion of a Christian kind, have firm faith in these truths. Happily, their hope of everlasting bliss in heaven is virtually confirmed by the many near death experi-

---

28 (Grand Rapids: Zondervan, 1994), 950-1.
29 *St Therese of Lisieux by Those Who Knew Her,* op. cit., 192.

ences which have been reported in recent years. Here is a composite example which incorporates elements from many different reports.

A man is dying and as he reaches the point of greatest physical distress, he hears himself pronounced dead by his doctor. He begins to hear an uncomfortable noise, a loud ringing or buzzing, and at the same time feels himself moving very rapidly through a long dark tunnel. After this, he suddenly finds himself outside of his own physical body, as though he is a spectator. He watches the resuscitation attempt from this unusual vantage point and is in a state of emotional upheaval.

After a while, he collects himself and becomes more accustomed to his condition. He notices that he still has a body but one of a very different nature and with very different powers from the physical body he has left behind. Soon other things begin to happen. Different people come to meet him. A loving, warm spirit of a kind he has never encountered before – a being of light – appears before him. This being asks him a question, in a nonverbal way which urges him to evaluate his deeds and helps him along by showing him an instantaneous playback of the major events of his life. He views these memories, not from the perspective he had when he experienced them, but rather from a third-person, empathic point of view. For instance, he takes the perspective, and senses the feelings of the person that he was unkind to. And if he sees an action where he was loving to someone he can feel the pleasurable feelings which his benevolence evoked in that person.

At a particular point he finds himself approaching some sort of barrier or border, apparently, representing the limit between this and the next life. Yet he finds he must go back to earth; the time for his death has not yet come. At this point he resists, for by now he is taken up with his attractive experiences in the afterlife and does not want to return. He is overwhelmed by intense feelings of joy, peace and love. Despite his inclination, he somehow reunites with his physical body and lives. Later on he tries to tell others, but has trouble doing so. In the first place he can find no human words adequate to describe those heavenly experiences. He also finds that because of the scepticism of his listeners he stops recounting what happened.

In 2014, scientists under the direction of Dr Sam Parnia at Southampton University completed the largest scientific study of near-death experiences. It was a four-year examination of 2,060 patients who had suffered cardiac arrest in hospitals in the U.S., U.K. and Austria. Among other things, the study recounted how one patient reported hearing two "bleeps" from a machine that sounded in three-minute intervals, revealing that he maintained awareness for more than three minutes after cardiac arrest. This patient was not only aware of sounds in the room, but was also able to accurately report with heightened visual acuity what was going on in the operating room. The events reported were verified by researchers after resuscitation. Dr Sam Parnia has written a book about the research entitled, *What Happens When We Die?*[30]. Studies like Parnia's indicate that Christians who developed a deep personal relationship with Jesus over the years, discover in Him a growing freedom from the fear of mortality. I have talked to a number of faith-filled Christians who have had positive near-death experiences, and without exception they told me that as a result they have no fear of death.

B] *THE ANTIDOTE TO THE FEAR OF GUILT AND CONDEMNATION*

When I was young the Irish Church tended to be Jansenistic and moralistic. As a number of our Irish novelists have pointed out, the lives of many people were blighted by morbid guilt feelings, and an exaggerated fear of hell. For example, in James Joyce's *Portrait of an Artist as a Young Man* we are told about a Jesuit priest who delivered a terrifying sermon on the subject of hell to school boys. "The horror of hell," he proclaimed, "is increased by its awful stench... some foul and putrid corpse that has lain rotting and decomposing in the grave, a jelly-like mass of liquid corruption... giving off dense choking fumes of nauseous loathsome decomposition. And then imagine this sickening stench, multiplied a millionfold and a millionfold again... a huge and rotting human fungus. Imagine all this, and you will have some idea of the horror of the stench of hell... O, how terrible is the

---

30   (Carlsbad, CA: Hay House, 2007).

lot of those wretched beings! The blood seethes and boils in the veins, the brains are boiling in the skull, the heart in the breast glowing and bursting, the bowels a red-hot mass of burning pulp, the tender eyes flaming like molten balls... The damned howl and scream at one another, their torture and rage intensified by the presence of beings tortured and raging like themselves... They are helpless and hopeless: it is too late now for repentance."[31] Clearly, this is a religion based on terror and not on love. And as St Paul reminded us in 1 Tim 2:7, "the spirit you received *is not a spirit of fear.*"

When she was a young person, St Therese of Lisieux had a neurotic fear of judgement and condemnation by God. Speaking about her Jansenistic preparation for the sacrament of confirmation she said, "What the priest told us was frightening. He spoke about mortal sin, and he described a soul in the state of sin and how much God hated it." At the age of 14 Therese had a profound religious experience of God's love at midnight Mass, Christmas 1886. Therese called it her night of conversion and illumination. "Charity had found its way into my heart," she declared, "calling on me to forget myself and simply do what God wanted of me." One result of Therese's experience of God's unconditional mercy and love was the fact that she lost her fear of being judged or condemned by God. She realised, in her heart of hearts that, "there is now no condemnation for those who are in Christ Jesus" (Rm 8:1) and that, "There is no fear in love. But perfect love drives out fear, *because fear has to do with punishment.* The one who fears is not made perfect in love" (1 Jn 4:18).

A number of years ago a nurse, in Bray, County Wicklow, rang me. She said that she was looking after a man who was dying from cancer and had asked to see me. So I drove to the town and met the man. He explained that he was a recovering alcoholic, that he hadn't long to live and was terrified of having to come before God as a just judge. He said that he had listened to a recording of a talk I had given about the mercy of God. Although he liked it very much he thought that it was too good

---

31   *A Portrait of the Artist as a Young Man* (London: Penguin, 2000), chapter three, section two.

to be true. He asked me if I could assure him that what I said was in accord with the teaching of the scriptures and the Church.

I can remember quoting Rm 8:1 to him, "There is therefore now no condemnation for those who are in Christ Jesus." Were you baptised? I asked. "Yes, I was baptised shortly after my birth." Well then, I replied, "you are in Christ in virtue of your baptism." Then I said that I wanted him to answer two questions. "Firstly, do you believe that Jesus Christ is Lord?" "Yes, of course I do," he replied. "And secondly, do you believe that God raised him from the dead?" Again, he answered with an emphatic, "Yes." "Well then," I replied, "listen to what St Paul says in Rom 10:9, 'if you confess with your mouth, "Jesus is Lord", and believe in your heart that God raised him from the dead, you will be saved.' So you see," I continued, "if you look only into the eyes of God's mercy, expecting only mercy, you will receive only mercy, now and at the moment of your death." When he responded by saying that he was afraid of having to undergo the purifying suffering of purgatory, I quoted something St Therese of Lisieux had said to one of her dying companions who had the same fear, "You do not have enough trust. You have too much fear before the good God. I can assure you that He is grieved over this. You should not fear Purgatory because of the suffering there, but should instead ask that you not deserve to go there in order to please God, who so reluctantly imposes this punishment. As soon as you try to please Him in everything and have an unshakable trust He purifies you every moment in His love and He lets no sin remain. And then you can be sure that you will not have to go to Purgatory."

When the man said that he did trust completely in God's mercy I heard his confession and gave him a general absolution. When I left him, he was completely at peace with God. He died two days later. When I attended his funeral, his nurse told me that from the time I left him to the moment of his death he had been completely free from fear. So, if you want to be freed from the fear of guilt and condemnation ask God to reveal the length and breadth, the height and depth of Christ's incomprehensible mercy and love to you through an outpouring of the Holy Spirit. Many people come into that liberating experience by attending such things as an Alpha Course or a Life in the Spirit Seminar.

C] *AN ANTIDOTE TO THE FEAR OF EMPTINESS AND MEANINGLESSNESS.*

It was mentioned earlier that we are living in a post-truth society. As a result, many people feel that they are adrift on a sea of relativity. British Journalist Bernard Levin wrote, "Countries like ours are full of people who have all the material comforts they desire, together with such non-material blessings as a happy family, and yet lead lives of quiet and, at times, noisy desperation, understanding nothing but the fact that there is a hole inside them. And however much food and drink they pour into it, however many motorcars and television sets they stuff it with, however many well-balanced children and loyal friends they parade around the edges of it, it aches."[32] In other words, they fear, like novelist Leo Tolstoy, that their desire for ultimate meaning will be frustrated and that their lives will have no real purpose.

The crucial issue of ultimate truth arose at the trial of Jesus. "Pilate said to him, 'So you are a king?' Jesus answered, 'You say that I am a king. For this purpose I was born and for this purpose I have come into the world - to bear witness to the truth. Everyone who is of the truth listens to my voice.' Pilate said to him, 'What is truth?'" (Jn 18:37-8). Pilate's question continues to reverberate in contemporary culture. The fact is, truth is not a proposition, it is a Person, the person of Jesus Christ. Speaking about himself he said, "I am... the truth" (Jn 14:6). On another occasion Jesus prayed to his Father, "Sanctify them in the truth" (Jn 17:17). So, if a person has a spiritual awakening of

---

32   From a newspaper column, 'Life's Great Riddle, and No Time to Find Its Meaning' quoted by Nicky Gumbel in *Questions of Life: An Opportunity to Explore the Meaning of Life* (London: Hodder & Stoughton, 2018), 11.

a Christian kind, e.g., as a result of baptism in the Spirit,[33] he or she comes to have an intimate relationship with the Lord who is Truth incarnate. For example, Tolstoy's crisis of faith came to an end when, having been edified by the simple faith of some peasants he knew, he overcame his rationalistic doubts and recovered his childhood sense of God. The result was dramatic: "Everything came alive, and took on meaning. The moment I thought I knew God, I lived. But the moment I forgot him, the moment I stopped believing, I stopped living.... To know God and to live are the same thing."[34]

---

33   "Baptism in the Spirit is a life-transforming experience of the love of God the Father poured into one's heart by the Holy Spirit, and received through a total surrender to the lordship of Jesus Christ. This grace brings alive sacramental baptism and confirmation, deepens communion with God and with fellow Christians, enkindles evangelistic fervour and equips a person with charisms for service and mission." *Baptism in the Holy Spirit* (Luton: New Life, 2012), 15.

34   Henri Troyat, *Tolstoy*, op. cit., 524.

CHAPTER FIVE

REALISTIC FEARS

Feelings are the fingerprints of subjectivity, at once similar to those of other people and nevertheless unique. They are the point of conscious intersection where our capacity for inwardness and relatedness meet. They put us in touch with two realms, the perceived world of external reality, and our own inner world. Our feelings appraise the outward world – this includes inward fantasies, memories and images, which are internalised versions of external things – and respond to them. Our feelings tell us inwardly whether the objects of our perception are agreeable or disagreeable, satisfying or dissatisfying, threatening or life affirming. Fear is a fundamental, God-given, defensive emotion. In English there are many words which describe different kinds and intensities of fear such as alarm, scared, worry, concern, misgiving, qualm, disquiet, uneasiness, wariness, nervousness, edginess, jitteriness, apprehension, anxiety, trepidation, fright, dread, anguish, panic, terror, horror, consternation, distress, unnerved, distraught, threatened and defensive.

The emotion or feeling of fear is our spontaneous and instinctive reaction to the perception of a threat of one kind or another. Pioneers in fear research, Caroline and Robert Blanchard are quoted as saying in Joseph Le Dough's *The Emotional Brain*, "If something occurs – a loud noise or sudden movement – people tend to respond immediately... stop what they are doing... orient toward the stimulus, and try to identify its potentiality for actual danger. This happens very quickly, in a reflex-like sequence in which action precedes any voluntary or consciously intentioned behaviour. A poorly localizable or identifiable threat source, such as a sound in the night, may elicit an active immobility so profound that the frightened person can hardly speak or even breathe. However, if the danger source has been localized and an avenue for flight or concealment is plausible, the person will probably try to flee or hide... Actual contact, particularly painful contact, with the threat source is also likely to elicit thrashing, biting, scratching and other potentially damaging activities by the terrified person."[35]

Realistic fears lead us, as the Blanchards point out, to defend ourselves from a perceived danger by activating the fight or flight reflex. Our bodies are readied either to escape from the danger, or equipped to meet it head on. So realistic fears are very helpful. For example, because I fear that I could fail my final exams, I study long and hard. Because I am afraid of getting the flu, and being absent from work, I get inoculated. Because I am afraid of fire, I install smoke alarms in my home and have a number of fire extinguishers about the house. Because I fear that my computer might crash, I back up my files on an external hard drive. Because I fear the bull that is charging towards me, I run away as fast as I can and jump over a fence to safety. In all these cases realistic fear leads to appropriate self-protective action. Sometimes, however, fear can have a paralysing effect on the will.

A] *IMAGINATION AND FEAR*

On one occasion before Christmas, many years ago, I felt very stressed. I was thinking of all the cards I had to write, the presents I had to buy, the trips I had to make, people I needed to contact either by phone or in person, events I needed to organise, new tyres I needed to get for the car etc. The thought of so many things that needed doing in such a short period of time caused me to panic. I thought to myself, "it is impossible. I will never be able to get so many things done in such a short time". The acute fear I experienced led to a kind of paralysis. I felt so overwhelmed by the sheer impossibility of accomplishing all the tasks that I was unable to do anything at all. It was as if I was saying to myself, "why start, it is all hopeless!" Then I remembered something that a colleague had told me some years before.

Apparently, he had gone to a barren area of North Africa for a time of prayer and reflection. When he arrived at his destination he

---

35   (New York: Phoenix, 1998), 131.

was met by a Little Brother of Charles de Foucauld. He told this colleague of mine that he would be on his own for most of his stay. He proffered this advice: "It is important that you live entirely in the present because that is the only moment where God is truly present. Your enemies will be the past and the future. Neither is real. The first, which is over, will try to invade the present moment by means of your memory, while the second, which is yet to come, will try to invade the present moment by means of your imagination. Resist the workings of both memory, which evokes guilt, and imagination, which evokes fear, in order to live in the grace of the present moment. This point reminded me of something Jesus said: "Therefore do not worry about tomorrow, for tomorrow will worry about itself. Each day has enough trouble of its own" (Mt 6:34). I also recalled something St Padre Pio prayed: "Lord, I commend my past to your mercy, my future to your providence, and my present to your love."

As soon as I recalled all this I tried to rein in my over-active imagination with the bridle and bit of reason and faith. I thought to myself, I'll write down all the things I have to do in their order of importance. Then I will begin to tackle the various tasks, one by one, starting right now. As soon as I disciplined and controlled my imagination in this way, I felt a new surge of hope and energy. My stress levels went down quickly. I began to carry out the nominated tasks in sequence. By living in the present, I found that I wasn't fearful of the future. In the event I got everything done much more quickly and efficiently than I had ever thought possible. But I learned a lesson. Stress can be fuelled by an imagination that gets out of hand by picturing all the scary things that might, or might not, happen in the future.

We can visualise all kinds of unpleasant possibilities which could befall us such as mental illness, cancer, betrayal, a debilitating stroke, humiliating failure, loss of one's job and income, bereavement, public disgrace etc. Needless to say, the thought of what could possibly befall us in the future can flood the present with all kinds of debilitating fears. Surely St Francis de Sales was correct when he said, "It will be quite enough to receive the evils which come upon us from time to time, without anticipating them by the imagination."[36]

B] *Fear in relationships*

Fear is very common in human relationships. When we were children the first developmental task we faced was whether to trust or mistrust our parents or carers. Our response depended on the quality and consistency of the love and care we experienced. If it seemed to be lacking, intermittent, or conditional, we limped out of childhood with low-self esteem, timidity and a compromised ability to trust other human beings. That fearful mistrust has knock on effects when we face the developmental challenge of forming intimate, trusting, committed relationships mainly between the ages of 20 and 40. Although people who are mistrustful may desire to be intimate by sharing their deepest thoughts and feelings with friends or lovers, they may refrain from doing so because of the fear of being misunderstood, ridiculed, hurt or rejected. So they fail to take the risk and opt for closeness rather than intimacy.[37] One of the characters in Iris Murdock's novel *Under the Net* says, "I hate solitude, but I'm afraid of intimacy. The substance of my life is a private conversation with myself which to turn into a dialogue would be equivalent to self-destruction. The company which I need is the company which a pub or a cafe will provide. I have never wanted a communion of souls. It's already hard enough to tell the truth to oneself."[38] People who fail to satisfy their intimacy needs will not only feel isolated, unloved, and frustrated, they will tend to displace their intimacy needs in the form of unhealthy attitudes and behaviours, e.g. drinking too much, hypochondria, obsessional behaviour etc. Scripture suggests that we can overcome this kind of fear by means of trust in God. The Lord has said, "Never will I leave you; never will I forsake you." So we say with confidence, "The

---

36 *Letters to Person in Religion*, 4, 2.
37 Cf. Pat Collins, C.M., *Intimacy and the Hungers of the Heart* (Dublin: Columba, 1992), 101.
38 (London: Vintage Books, 2002), 34.

Lord is my helper; I will not be afraid. What can mere mortals do to me?" (Heb 13:5-6).

Over the years I have been fortunate to have had a few good women friends but fear had often blunted my longing to share deeply and honestly with them. Frequently, I found myself torn between two conflicting desires. On the one hand I longed to tell them the whole truth about myself while on the other I experienced an inhibiting fear that, if I did so, they would turn against me. However, I can remember a graced occasion when I visited one of those friends. Things got off to a good start when I found myself revealing lots of embarrassing and shameful truths about my past life, which I had never told anyone before. Having listened with great empathy, at one point she went out to the kitchen, to make two cups of coffee. When I was alone I felt content, but irrational fear led me to think, "Quit now while you are still winning". But when my friend returned, mysteriously courage overrode my usual fear and I continued to share deeply with her. By the end of the conversation, it was evident that instead of alienating me from my friend, my honest self disclosure had enabled us to move from closeness to a deeper emotional intimacy than ever before. That moment of breakthrough was one of the most important of my life.

C] *FEAR OF CHANGE*

Change has always been a characteristic of human life. As the Greek philosopher Heraclitus (535 – c. 475 BC) said, "No man ever steps in the same river twice, for it's not the same river and he's not the same man." Poet Alfred Lord Tennyson added, "The old order changeth, yielding place to new, And God fulfils Himself in many ways, Lest one good custom should corrupt the world."[39] We are living at a time when the rate of change is accelerating at an unprecedented pace. It makes considerable demands on all of us while often evoking emotional fear and resistance. But as Cardinal, John Henry Newman reminded us, "To live is to change,

---

39 "The Passing of Arthur," from *Idylls of the King*, lines 45-50.

and to be perfect is to have changed often."[40] But change can be painful and demanding. For example, in par. 168 of his Apostolic Exhortation on holiness, *Rejoice and be Glad*, Pope Francis wrote, "the forces of evil induce us not to change, to leave things as they are, to opt for a rigid resistance to change. Yet that would be to block the working of the Spirit". In pars. 27- 33. of his Apostolic Exhortation *The Joy of the Gospel*, Pope Francis talked about the challenge of changing from maintenance to mission in parishes. He observed, that the conversion of church structures which this change would necessitate can evoke fearful resistance in priests and lay people alike. Often, they will be the victims of what is referred to nowadays as groupthink, i.e. when members of a community insulate themselves from outside opinions. Not surprisingly, as Pope Francis points out, "they will say such things as, 'We have always done things this way.' I invite everyone to be bold and creative in this task of rethinking the goals, structures, style and methods of evangelisation."

Rosabeth Kanter Moss, professor of business at Harvard Business School cites 10 reasons why people resist change.[41]

1. *Loss of control* – Change done by us is exciting. Change done to us is threatening.

2. *Excess uncertainty* – Change feels dangerous when there is not enough information about what is or will be happening.

3. *Surprises* – Without time to assimilate and absorb, news of change is threatening.

4. *The "difference" effect* – Change requires questioning of familiar routines and habits, while adjusting to new people, norms and environment.

5. *Loss of face* – Shame for and blaming of the former way of doing things; this can cause divisiveness.

---

40   "The Development of Ideas" in *Development of Christian Doctrine,* chapter one.

41   https://utopianfrontiers.com/rosabeth-moss-kanter-ten-reasons-people-resist-change/

6. *Concerns about future competence* – "Will I be able to meet new expectations?" Personal doubt, risk of appearing/feeling foolish.

7. *Ripple effects* – Disruptions due to the change.

8. *More work* – Change requires more energy, time, and preoccupation. Going "above and beyond" is often required during intense periods of change.

9. *Past resentments* – Simmering resentments are jarred loose by change. Aggrieved members may not go along with what leadership wants.

10. *Sometimes the threat is real* – Sometimes the rumour mill is right: jobs, etc. are at risk; the leadership may have an unspoken agenda.

Like Pope Francis, leaders of all types of secular and religious organisations find that one of the skills they most need is an ability to assuage fears while facilitating a process of courageous adaptation and transformation in secular and religious organisations.

Fear of change and a desire to stick to the *status quo,* in the belief that the devil you know is better than the devil you don't know, can have a debilitating effect. To progress in life all of us need to be prepared to take risks by moving from our comfort zones. As the saying goes, "He who never undertook anything never achieved anything." In our daily lives we encounter all kinds of opportunities and challenges. I know that in the past people have invited me to do many demanding tasks. Although I found many of them to be attractive and exciting, I was often afraid because of such things as the amount of work involved, the possibility of failure, having to launch into the deep, or biting off more than I could chew etc. So frequently I avoided such opportunities in the name of a false prudence, while in fact the real motive behind my cautious choices was a self-centred, cowardly type of fear. When I became aware of the inhibiting effect of fear in my life, I could see that it was preventing me, in many instances, from doing the will of God. So I began to appreciate how important the virtue of courage is in Christian spirituality. Yes, it is natural to feel afraid, but in the name of boldness, we need to ensure that we are not mastered by it. As St Paul said to Timothy, "God did not give us a spirit of timidity *or* cowardice *or* fear" (2 Tim 1:7 *Amplified Bible*).

CHAPTER SIX

COPING WITH REALISTIC FEARS

Fear is a God given emotion that alerts us to possible dangers while energising us either to flee or fight. But we have to be careful not to let fear get out of control in such a way that instead of enhancing the quality of our lives, it diminishes it. Over the years I have found that two things help me to keep my realistic fears in check, firstly, trust in the providence of God, and secondly, the gift of a God-granted courage.

TRUSTING IN THE PROVIDENCE OF GOD

One of the consequences of knowing Jesus as the Truth and listening to the truth of his words is that the person develops a strong sense of divine providence. Jesus believed that God has a *benevolent plan* for each of our lives. He agreed with Jeremiah who said: "For surely I know the plans I have for you, says the Lord, plans for your welfare and not for harm, to give you a future and a hope" (Jer 29:11). That plan is expressed in three interrelated ways.

Firstly, there is one's vocation in life whether married or single. For example, I discovered mine when, as a result of a religious experience at the age of 18, I decided to become a priest in 1963.

Secondly, one can discover a vocation within a vocation, e.g. a married man who feels and responds to a call to the diaconate.

Thirdly, within the context of our vocation we are guided by the Spirit on a day-to-day basis (cf. Gal 5:18). As Cardinal Newman wrote: "Lead kindly light amid the encircling gloom…. I do not ask to see the distant scene, one step enough for me." I have written about this important topic in my Guided by God: Ordinary and Charismatic Ways of Discovering God's Will.42

Jesus also taught that besides having a plan for our lives, God

---

42   (Luton: New Life Publishing, 2015).

provides for us in our needs. That provision is experienced in two interrelated ways;

Firstly, internally in the form of natural talents and God-given graces. If God calls a person to some task, e.g. to be a preacher and teacher, he gives them such things as a good education, retentive memory and good communication skills. God will also supply the ordinary and extraordinary graces needed to carry out the task.

Secondly, God's provision is experienced in external ways, by means of secondary causes, i.e. not directly by God, but by means of people and events, in the form of material benefits. As Jesus said: "You must not set your hearts on things to eat and things to drink; nor must you worry. It is the gentiles of this world who set their hearts on all these things. Your Father well knows you need them. Now set your hearts on his kingdom, and these other things will be given you as well" (Lk 12:30). St Vincent de Paul once said: "We ought to have confidence in God that he will look after us since we know for certain that as long as we are grounded in that sort of love and trust we will always be under the protection of God in heaven, we will remain unaffected by evil and never lack what is needed when everything seems headed for disaster."43 Normally God helps us in non-magical ways by means of secondary causes such as coincidences, apparent good luck, etc. Occasionally we may be helped directly by God by means of a healing or miracle.

Whenever a person knows Jesus as the Truth and has a strong sense of the providential plan and provision of God, not only for the Church but also for his or her own life, an anxious and fearful sense of apprehension is replaced by a profound sense of meaning, purpose and hope. That said, surely philosopher John Murray was correct when he said, "The maxim of illusory religion runs: 'Fear not; trust in God and he will see that none of the things you fear will happen to you;' that of real religion, on the contrary, is: 'Fear not; the things

43 St Vincent de Paul, "Common Rules of The Congregation of the Mission" in *Constitutions and Statutes of the Congregation of the Mission* (Rome: General Curia of the CM, 1984), 108.

that you are afraid of are quite likely to happen to you, but they are nothing to be afraid of'."[44] Here is a well known prayer of abandonment to divine providence which was written by Charles de Foucauld (1858-1916):

> "Father, I abandon myself into your hands; do with me what you will. Whatever you may do, I thank you: I am ready for all, I accept all. Let only your will be done in me, and in all your creatures - I wish no more than this, O Lord. Into your hands I commend my soul: I offer it to you with all the love of my heart, for I love you, Lord, and so need to give myself, to surrender myself into your hands without reserve, and with boundless confidence, for you are my Father."

THE GIFT OF COURAGE

The 2017 movie *The Darkest Hour* recounts how British prime minister Winston Churchill had to confront so many crises and threats at the beginning of World War II. It recalled how, in spite of his propensity to suffer from depression, he had immense courage as a leader, and refused to negotiate terms with Hitler even though his country was in danger of being invaded and a number of his cabinet colleagues were strongly urging him to appease the Fuhrer. Churchill knew what he was talking about when he said that, "Fear is a reaction. Courage is a decision," and "Courage is the first of human qualities because it is the quality that guarantees all the others." How true!

Courage is an outstanding Christian virtue. Remember how the first disciples had been commissioned by Jesus to make disciples of all the nations. Following Pentecost, the apostles overcame their fears and courageously preached the Good News about Jesus to their fellow Jews. But before long they experienced persecution. Peter and John were jailed. So, not surprisingly, the apostles were afraid that they might be martyred. When the two men escaped from prison

---

44 From the Gifford Lectures 1953-4, quoted by William Barry, S.J., *Paying Attention to God* (Notre Dame: Ave Maria Press, 1990), 29.

in a miraculous way, they returned to the community of believers. Then they prayed, "Enable your servants to speak your word with great boldness" (Acts 4:29). The word "boldness" in Greek is *parrhesia* which means "courageous speech". Then we are told that, "After they prayed, the place where they were meeting was shaken. And they were all filled with the Holy Spirit and spoke the word of God boldly" (Acts 4:31).

In Eph 6:20 Paul said, "Pray that I may declare the gospel fearlessly, as I should." In 2 Tim 1:7-8 Paul said to Timothy, his protégé, "God did not give us a spirit of timidity, but a spirit of power, of love and of self-discipline. So do not be ashamed to testify about our Lord."

Commenting on the need for *parrhesia,* Pope Francis has written in par. 133 *On the Call to Holiness in Today's World,* "We need the courage the Spirit gives, lest we be paralysed by fear and excessive caution, lest we grow used to keeping within safe bounds. Let us remember that closed spaces grow musty and unhealthy."

Prayer for Christian courage is underpinned by the promises of God in the scriptures. For instance, Paul assured us in Phil 2:13 that, "it is God who works in you, both to will and to work for his good pleasure". Three important assertions are made here:

- God is at work in you
- God is at work within you to enable you to know and to embrace God's will
- God who is at work within you by the power of the Holy Spirit, will enable you to work for his good pleasure by carrying out the divine will no matter how difficult it may seem to be. As St Paul testified in Phil 4:13, "I can do all things through him who strengthens me." So there is no need to be mastered by fear.

When we claim the promises of scripture in this way, by means of expectant faith, we may continue to feel the fear while going on courageously to do the divine will nevertheless.

A prayer for overcoming fear

Heavenly Father, my heart and mind are flooded with fears.
Sometimes I am paralysed, I feel unable to go on.
These fears are overwhelming, they remain with me day and night.
Yet I hold onto your truth.
You have told us not to fear, for you have overcome the world.
So I cling to you, I trust in your promises, that you will never fail
me, never forsake me.
In moments of such crippling fear,
I choose to trust in you.
I know you have experienced the most fearful situations,
I know that you have risen again.
In you all promises meet and find their fulfilment.
You are my Saviour,
I hide in you, protected by your love,
And sheltered by your grace.
Grant me the courage to do your will,
No matter what difficulties I may face. Amen.

CHAPTER SEVEN

NEUROTIC FORMS OF ANXIETY, FEAR & PHOBIA

In chapter two, on existential anxiety and fear, it was suggested that the deepest need of the human being is a sense of ultimate purpose and unconditional meaning. Some psychologists such as Frankl, Jung and Maslow maintained that if a person failed to discover purpose and meaning in life he or she would tend to develop anxieties and fears of a neurotic kind. Unlike existential anxiety, which is natural and realistic in a contingent and threatening world, neurotic anxiety is unrealistic and unhealthy. According to Jung the self archetype is the one which orientates, directs and enables the healthy development of the psyche so that the person increasingly achieves the goal of individuation, i.e. becoming what one truly is. Otherwise, instead of becoming whole, the personality will become divided and neurotic. In section two of this book, which deals with addiction, I will refer to what Frankl, Jung and Maslow had to say about the connection between neurosis and a failure to develop a sense of ultimate meaning and self-actualisation as a result of having peak experiences of a transcendent, religious kind. As Italian psychiatrist, Roberto Assagioli (1888-1974), once wrote, "The experience of super-conscious reality cancels out fear, for any sense of fear is incompatible with a realisation of the fullness and permanence of life."[45] There are many causes and forms of neurotic anxiety. It is a huge and complex subject. Because of a lack of space we will only take a cursory look at the topic.

A] *ANXIETY DISORDERS*

Anxiety disorders are a group of responses characterised by significant feelings of apprehension and fear. More often than not, anxiety is a worry about possible future events whereas fear is a reaction to current events. These feelings may cause psychosomatic symp-

---

45   *Transpersonal Development* (London: Crucible, 1991), 29.

toms, such as a fast heart rate, rapid breathing and trembling. There are a number of anxiety disorders including:

- A generalised anxiety disorder is characterised by excessive, uncontrollable and often irrational worry, that is, apprehensive expectation about future events or activities.

- A specific phobia is any kind of anxiety disorder that amounts to an unreasonable or irrational fear related to exposure to specific objects, situations or stimuli, e.g. spiders, or enclosed spaces. As a result, the affected person tends to avoid contact with the intimidating objects or situations and, in severe cases, any mention or depiction of them.

- A social anxiety disorder is the fear of situations which involve interaction with other people. You could say that this disorder is the fear and anxiety of being negatively judged and evaluated by others. It is a pervasive disorder and causes anxiety and fear in most areas of a person's life.

- A separation anxiety disorder is one in which an individual experiences excessive anxiety regarding separation from home or from people to whom the individual has a strong emotional attachment (e.g. a parent, caregiver, significant other or spouse).

- Agoraphobia is a type of anxiety disorder in which a person fears and avoids places or situations that might cause him or her to panic while feeling trapped, helpless or embarrassed, e.g. leaving one's home to go to the supermarket.

- Panic disorder is a form of anxiety characterised by recurrent unexpected panic attacks which are sudden periods of intense fear that can include palpitations, sweating, shaking, shortness of breath, numbness or a feeling that something really catastrophic is going to happen.

- Selective mutism is a complex childhood anxiety disorder characterised by a child's inability to speak and communicate effectively in select social settings, such as school. These children are often only able to speak and communicate in settings where they are comfortable, secure and relaxed.

People often have more than one anxiety disorder. The causes of their apprehension are usually a combination of genetic, traumatic and environmental factors. Anxiety disorders can often occur together with other mental problems such as depression, bi-polar disorder and low self-esteem. To be properly diagnosed, symptoms typically need to be present for at least six months. Without treatment, anxiety disorders tend to persist. Treatment may include lifestyle changes, counselling and medications such as antidepressants, benzodiazepines or beta blockers.

B] AN UNHEALTHY SUPEREGO AND FEAR OF GOD

Because of having an unhealthy superego, many Christians can have a negative image of God.[46] Let me explain. When a child is very small, it is totally helpless and dependant on its parents or parental substitutes for such things as clothes, food, shelter and love. The child is a bundle of undisciplined and selfish needs and desires. In an effort to socialise the child, its parents have to discipline it. In doing so they may give the child the impression in verbal and non-verbal ways that they will love it more *if* it behaves… *if* it doesn't urinate on the carpet… *if* it doesn't put jam on the wallpaper… *if* it doesn't cry too much, etc. Although the child desires to do its "own thing" it desires the apparently conditional love of its parents even more. So it learns to conform in order to retain the affection and acceptance of the parent/s.

As the child develops, it begins to internalise the values and attitudes of its parents, in the form of conscience. This is what Freud referred to as the superego. In the case of an unhealthy superego, however, the person's conscience says, usually in an unconscious way, you can only love and accept yourself if you do what you "ought", "should," or "have" to do. Some people have referred to this propensity as "hardening of the oughteries". The demands of conscience often become synonymous with the demands of God. As a result, if either the growing child or an adult indulges in any for-

---

46 Cf., Pat Collins, "Healthy and Unhealthy Forms of Guilt" in *The Joy of Belonging* (Galway: Campus, 1993), 31-35.

bidden instinctual behaviour, e.g. of a selfish or sexual kind, the un-healthy superego may say, "Because you did such a bad thing, you are a bad person, you can no longer love or accept yourself, and the same is true of God, God doesn't accept or love you either." This fear of self-alienation and separation from God evokes a strong feeling of acute anxiety. In his book, *Man Becoming*, the late Gregory Baum referred to this point when he wrote, "The idea of God as judge on a throne, meting out punishment, corresponds to a self-destructive trend of the human psyche. The person who is dominated by his su-perego—and no one is able to escape it altogether - has the accuser, judge and tormentor all wrapt in one, built into his own psychic makeup. When such a person hears the Christian message with the accent on God the judge, he can project his superego on the divinity and then use religion as an instrument to subject himself to this court and, unknown to himself, to promote his own unconscious self-hatred... Jesus has come to save men from their superego. God is not a punisher; God saves."[47]

C] *IRRATIONAL PHOBIAS*

In a book entitled, *An Outline of Psychiatry*, Clarence Rowe M.D. says, "phobias are persistent, obsessive fears of specific objects, ac-tivities, or situations. Examples include fear of height, closed spac-es, open spaces, strangers, animals, dirt, or school. Certain fears, as of harmless bugs and snakes, are extremely common, and not considered pathological, but phobias are typically found in phobic disorders."[48] The following Old Testament passage is full of anxiety and phobic fear, "Among those nations you will find no repose, no resting place for the sole of your foot. There the Lord will give you an anxious mind, eyes weary with longing, and a despairing heart. You will live in constant suspense, filled with dread both night and day, never sure of your life. In the morning you will say, "If only it

---

47 (New York: Herder & Herder Inc., reprinted by permission of Harper Collins Publishers, 1970), 223.
48 (Dubuque, Iowa: Wm. C. Brown Company, 1980), 36.

were evening!" and in the evening, "If only it were morning!" — because of the terror that will fill your hearts and the sights that your eyes will see" (Deut 28:65-68).

CHAPTER EIGHT

OVERCOMING NEUROTIC ANXIETY, FEAR & PHOBIA

This chapter takes a brief look at neurotic forms of anxiety and fear. Because it is a technical topic which is best dealt with by psychologists and psychotherapists, I will not have much to say here about the in-depth dimensions involved. However, I will look briefly at these topics from the perspective of Christian spirituality.

A] COPING WITH NEUROTIC ANXIETY

Although the subject of anxiety states is a big one, ways of overcoming them will not be proposed here because it is a complex topic, mainly psychological in nature, and beyond the limited scope of this book. I have a conviction, however, that what was said about existential anxiety is very relevant at this point, because often neurotic anxiety and phobias are the result of unacknowledged and unresolved existential anxiety. Carl Jung maintained that people would not overcome their neurotic anxiety disorders until they had genuine religious experience. In an essay entitled, "Psychotherapists or the Clergy" in *Psychology and Western Religion*, he wrote, "In thirty years I have treated many patients in the second half of life (i.e. over 35). Every one of them became ill because he or she had lost that which the living religions in every age have given their followers, (i.e. religious experience) and none of them was fully healed who did not regain his religious outlook."[49] Research has confirmed the fact that people who are intrinsically religious and who engage in spiritual practices such as contemplative meditation, and receive prayer for inner healing, suffer from less neurotic anxiety and fear.[50] This is

---

49   (London: Ark:1988), 202.
50   Cf. Pat Collins, CM., "Is Prayer Good for Your Health?" in *The Broken Image* (Dublin: Columba, 2002), 86-99.

probably the outcome of the fact that the individual self has escaped from the prison of excessive self-reference by becoming absorbed, in a self-forgetful way, in the greater reality of God. More will be said about this point in the section on overcoming addictions.

B] COPING WITH AN UNHEALTHY SUPEREGO

People who have a morbid fear of God because of having an unhealthy superego can do a number of things to break into the freedom of the children of God.

- Try to become aware of the activity of the unhealthy superego in your life.
- Avoid asking what you "ought," "must," or "have" to do. In the light of your relationship with the Lord and other people ask yourself what it is that you "want", "desire", or, "yearn" to do as a result of a sense of inner conviction.
- In prayer focus on the unconditional love of God. St Teresa of Avila used to encourage people to imagine that Jesus was standing in front of them looking at them. Then she would say, "notice that he is looking at you with eyes full of love and humility." Then listen to these words, "Jesus Christ, the Risen Lord who is present, loves and accepts you just as you are... You don't have to change to get his love. You don't have to become better... to get out of your sinful ways... He obviously wants you to become better. He clearly wants you to give up your sin. But you do not have to do this to get his love and his acceptance. That you have already, right now, just as you are, even before you decide to change, and whether you decide to change or not... Do you believe this?... Take your time over it... Then decide whether you believe it or not."[51] Try to see moral values in terms of conscious relationship with God, rather than in terms of impersonal laws.

....

51 "The Heart of Christ" in *Sadhana a Way to God* (Gujarat: Anand Press, 1983), 114-115.

- If you are going to confession, ask God who searches every heart to search yours to help you to know your sin, i.e. the areas in your life where you failed to receive the unconditional love God was offering you, or failed to love others in the way God was loving you.
- Ask the Lord for the grace of perfect contrition, i.e. being sorry for your sins, not because you have a morbid fear that God has withdrawn conditional love from you, but because you have selfishly withdrawn your love from the Lord of unconditional love.

Many people suffer from neurotic fear because of the hurts and deprivations of the past. For instance, in recent years I have run workshops on the topic of healing the father wound. Pope Benedict adverted to the problem of the absent father, whether physically or emotionally, when he said in January 2013, "It is not always easy today to talk about fatherhood. Especially in our Western world, broken families, increasingly absorbing work commitments, concerns, and often the fatigue of trying to balance the family budget, the distracting invasion of the mass media in daily life are some of the many factors that can prevent a peaceful and constructive relationship between fathers and their children. At times communication becomes difficult, trust can be lost and relationship with the father figure can become problematic. Even imagining God as a father becomes difficult, not having had an adequate model of reference. For those who have had the experience of an overly authoritarian and inflexible father, or an indifferent father lacking in affection, or even an absent father, it is not easy to think of God as Father and trustingly surrender oneself to Him." During the workshops I stress three points.

- Firstly, the need to be realistic about whether one's father was physically or emotionally absent or even abusive for one reason or another.
- Secondly, the need for the person to be willing, with God's help, to forgive his or her father for the hurt he caused by his absence or abuse.

- Thirdly, a person suffering from the father wound and the orphan spirit can ask for prayer for inner healing.

If one follows these three steps, not only will self-confidence and peace of mind increase, anxiety and fear will decrease. Over the years people have asked me whether there is a mother wound? The answer is yes. For example, for one reason or another a child may suffer emotionally due to a partial or total failure to form a trusting attachment with his or her mother. But it is too big a subject to deal with here. Suffice it to say that I have dealt with it indirectly elsewhere.[52]

C] COPING WITH PHOBIAS

I don't want to say much about overcoming phobic reactions. Like the subject of anxiety states, it is as big a topic which is more psychological than spiritual. Suffice it to say that there are different forms of cure that can be employed by therapists of different kinds.

- Flooding is a form of behaviour therapy used to treat people with fears or phobias. In flooding, the person with the fear is exposed to the thing that frightens them for a sustained period of time. The idea behind it is that, by exposing you to your fear, you will eventually see it as less fear-producing. For example, a therapist may take a person who is afraid of dogs into a kennel to expose him or her to a large number of dogs in a controlled situation.
- Desensitisation is not unlike flooding. It is employed by behaviour therapists to "desensitise" clients by exposing them to an anxiety-eliciting stimulus such as a phobic object, e.g. a spider or blood. The premise is that repeated exposures will eventually reduce or extinguish the fear. This process is called therapeutic exposure. Many therapists would agree that this approach is an effective treatment for several anxiety disorders.

---

52 Pat Collins, C.M., "Self-esteem and the Love of God," in *Growing in Health and Grace* (Galway: Campus, 1992), 27-43.

- Paradoxical intention was proposed by Viktor Frankl. On this subject see his, "Paradoxical Intention: A Logotherapeutic Technique" in *Psychotherapy and Existentialism*.[53] Frankl argued that people can overcome their anticipatory fear, e.g. of blushing, fainting, hiccuping, etc. by good humouredly reversing their intention. The method is successful because it utilises the human capacity for self-detachment. By laughing at oneself, the person puts a distance between him or herself and the symptom. Let me give an example. When I was a secondary school teacher, class could be disrupted by a pupil who was hiccuping in a loud, uncontrollable way. Inevitably the attention of classmates focused on the pupil with the problem. Some would crack jokes, others would slap him on the back while others would supply him with good advice. On a number of occasions, I overcame the problem by trying to reverse the victim's intention. I would take out all the money I had in my wallet, put it on the table in front of me and say, "hiccup one more time and you can have all that money!" The hiccuper would look at me and the money with utter surprise. He would try to hiccup again, urged on by his fellow pupils, but all to no avail. No one ever was able to take my money.

I'd have to admit, however, that phobias are notoriously difficult to cure and sometimes when one particular phobia seems to be cured it is replaced by another.

---

53   (London: Pelican, 1973), 136-154.

CHAPTER NINE

CONCLUSION

At a cursory glance there seems to be two opposing points of view in the Bible where fear is concerned. On the one hand we read in Prov 9:10 that, "The fear of the Lord is the beginning of wisdom," while in Deut 1:21 the Lord says, "Do not be afraid; do not be discouraged." The tension between the two verses is more apparent than real. By "fear of the Lord," the Book of Proverbs is not saying that a person should be apprehensive before a God who is wrongly thought to be distant, demanding and harsh. In this Bible verse the verb to fear means, not only to be full of awe and reverence in the awareness of God's tremendous majesty but also to be open to divine grace. When the person becomes aware of the compassion and benevolence of God, he or she will recognise that there is no need to be anxious about anything. As Jesus said to his followers, "I tell you, do not be anxious about your life, what you will eat or what you will drink, nor about your body, what you will put on. Is not life more than food, and the body more than clothing? Look at the birds of the air: they neither sow nor reap nor gather into barns, and yet your heavenly Father feeds them. Are you not of more value than they?" (Mt 6:25-6). St Paul echoed that sentiment in Phil 4:6 when he wrote, "do not be anxious about anything, but in everything by prayer and supplication with thanksgiving let your requests be made known to God".

When one reads the Bible, it is quite striking how often the word of God counsels people not to be afraid. I saw a suggestion on the internet that there are 145 instances. I would like to quote some examples from both the Old and the New Testaments. It is important to appreciate the fact that rather than being a form of advice, the Lord's words are commands which we should seek to obey while relying on divine grace to do so.

1. "Have I not commanded you? Be strong and courageous. **Do not be terrified**; do not be discouraged, for the Lord your God will be with you wherever you go". (Josh 1:9)

2. "This is what the Lord says to you: '**Do not be afraid or discouraged** because of this vast army. For the battle is not yours, but God's". (2 Chron 20:15)

3. And Moses said to the people, "**Fear not, stand firm**, and see the salvation of the Lord, which he will work for you today". (Ex 14:13)

4. "For now I have no strength, and no breath is left in me. Again one having the appearance of a man touched me and strengthened me. And he said: "Oh, man greatly beloved, **fear not**, peace be with you; be strong and of good courage". (Dan 10:17-20)

5. "Tell everyone who is discouraged, Be strong and **don't be afraid!** God is coming to your rescue". (Is 35:4)

6. "Peace is what I leave with you; it is my own peace that I give you. I do not give it as the world does. **Do not be worried and upset; do not be afraid**". (Jn 14:27)

7. "**Cast all your anxieties on the Lord** because he cares about you". (1 Pt 5:7)

8. "Immediately he spoke to them and said, 'Take courage! It is I. **Don't be afraid'**." (Mark 6:50)

In my book, *Encountering Jesus,* I included a final chapter about having Christian courage. Among other things, it recounted how in the early 1980s I lived in Boston, USA.[54] During my time there I experienced an extended time of challenge which caused me to be afraid. On one occasion I went to a Jesuit retreat centre in Weston, Massachusetts, to attend a directed retreat. It didn't go well and I felt very disheartened. One evening as I lay on my bed I tried to pray. Suddenly, an image came into my mind. I could see a dimly lit cave. There was a rock in the middle upon which rested an open

---

54   (Luton: New Life, 2017).

book. Immediately I thought to myself, "that's the Bible, if I read what it says on its open pages, God will speak to me". But when I approached the book, I was disappointed and frustrated to find that its pages were blank! I can remember saying to the Lord, "Why do you refuse to speak to me in this darkness?" A few minutes later I thought I heard an inner voice saying to me, "I will speak to you. Read Is 41:10." At first I was sceptical, feeling that this was a false inspiration, an example of wishful thinking on my part. However, after a prayer for God's help I opened the Bible and read these words, "fear not, for I am with you, be not dismayed, for I am your God; I will strengthen you, I will help you, I will uphold you with my victorious right arm." It proved to be very relevant at the time. While those words didn't console me in an emotional sense, they gave me the strength to keep going. As Ps 23:4 puts it, "Even though I walk through the valley of the shadow of death, I will fear no evil, for you are with me; your rod and your staff [the words and Spirit of God], they comfort me."

Do not be afraid

Over the years I have often reflected on Is 41:10 when I have been tempted to be anxious or afraid. Although all of us need to acknowledge our existential, neurotic and everyday fears, we should not be mastered by our feelings but act instead in accordance with the objective word and will of God. Is 41:10 begins with the words "fear not, for I am with you; be not dismayed". As I have already mentioned, these are not words of advice. Rather they are words of command. When the scriptures say to us "forgive one another" (Eph 4:20) we say with the poet Alexander Pope, "To err is human to forgive divine." But we know from experience that if we make the decision to do the impossible by forgiving, the Holy Spirit comes upon us and enables us to cross over from un-forgiveness to for-giveness. It is no different when it comes to fear. If we make the decision to be courageous, God's grace will enable us to defy our fears and to do the divine will.

The Lord makes four infallible and reassuring promises in Is 41:10.

- He begins by saying, "I Am with you," "I am your God." This is a very evocative assurance. When Moses asked God who he was, he replied, "I am who Am" (Ex 3:14). There is a New Testament echo of that sentiment in John's Gospel where Jesus made seven "I am" statements, e.g. "when he was asked if he was the king of the Jews, Jesus answered, "You are right in saying I AM" (Jn 18:37). The great "I am" is the One who is always with us in the person of Jesus.

- "I will strengthen you." This verse reminds me of a number of St Paul's paradoxical statements, such as, "My grace is sufficient for you, for my power is made perfect in weakness. Therefore, I will boast all the more gladly about my weaknesses, so that Christ's power may rest on me." (2 Cor 12:9) In Phil 4:13 he says, "I can do all things through Christ who strengthens me".

- "I will help you." This promise is reminiscent of Heb 13:5-6 which reads, "God has said, 'Never will I leave you; never will I forsake you.' So we say with confidence, 'The Lord is my helper; *I will not be afraid.* What can man do to me?'"

- "I will uphold you with my victorious right hand." I like the word "victorious" here. The Lord who is the victor will uphold us as we trust in God. In 2 Chron 20:15 we read, "the battle is not yours, but God's," and in Zech 4:6, "'Not by might nor by power, but by my Spirit,' says the Lord Almighty."

FROM PARANOIA TO METANOIA

In his *Introduction to the Devout Life,* part IV, chapter 11, St Francis de Sales wrote, "Anxiety is the greatest evil that can befall a soul, except sin." Fr Ron Rolheiser pointed out in one of his articles that Jesus' first proclamation was, "The time is at hand, repent and believe the good news." He went on to say that in Greek the word for repent is *metanoia,* a "word that literally means to do a 180-degree turn". But then he asks, "what are we to turn from?" "In Greek," he responds, "the word *metanoia* makes something of a pun (in terms of opposites) with the word paranoia. *Metanoia* is unparanoia. Hence what Jesus is saying at the beginning of the Gospel might be put something like this: "Become unparanoid and believe that it is good news!" Not surprisingly, therefore, having finished reciting the Lord's Prayer at Mass, we continue by saying, "Deliver us, Lord, from every evil, and grant us peace in our day. In your mercy keep us free from sin and *protect us from all anxiety* as we wait in joyful hope for the coming of our Saviour, Jesus Christ." Commenting on that prayer, Fr Rolheiser has suggested that it could be translated as follows, "Protect us, Lord, from going through life with a chip on our shoulders, angry at the world, full of paranoia, looking for someone to blame for our unhappiness." Amen to that!

PART TWO

FREEDOM FROM ADDICTION

CHAPTER TEN

INTRODUCTION

The origin of words can be fascinating and revealing. In English, the term 'addiction' comes from the Latin *ad,* meaning 'to', and *dicere,* which literally means to 'say' or 'pronounce.' Apparently, the word can be traced back to the Roman courts, where a judge could pronounce that a person was being handed over into the power and control of someone else, who would be his lord and master. Therefore we suffer from an addiction when we lose our inner freedom by falling under the power and control of some created thing. In his fine book, *Addiction and Grace,* Christian psychiatrist Gerald May defined an addiction as "any compulsive, habitual behaviour that limits the freedom of human desire. It is caused by attachment, or nailing down, of desire to specific objects."[55] Arguably there are two main kinds of addiction, substance and behavioural.

A] HERE IS A SAMPLE LIST OF SOME ADDICTIVE SUBSTANCES:

Cocaine, tobacco, heroin, prescription drugs, e.g. sedatives, sleeping pills and tranquillisers, alcohol, cannabis (marijuana), amphetamines, hallucinogens, inhalents, and other psychoactive drugs.

B] HERE IS A LIST OF SOME BEHAVIOURAL ADDICTIONS

- Eating addictions/disorders such as anorexia and bulimia. Statistics indicate that 61% of the members of Overeating Anonymous come from disturbed, alcoholic families.
- Sex/pornography addiction. It is estimated that about one in twelve of the adult population suffers from a sex addiction of one kind or another, e.g. compulsive infidelity or a preoccupation with pornography. For the sex addict, the reproductive system is transformed into a way of altering

55   (San Francisco: Harper & Row, 1988), 24.

one's mood. It is no longer the basis for creative and loving relationships; it is used for itself alone. For the addict, sex is a painful and humiliating experience, devoid of genuine pleasure. There is an excellent movie about the sadness of such sex addiction entitled, Shame, starring Michael Fassbender (2011). It is thought that sex addictions, like a number of other kinds of addiction, causes opiate type chemicals like endorphins to be secreted in the brain. It has been established that many of these addicts were sexually abused in childhood. Some psychologists have argued that over 80% of inappropriate sexual fantasy and activity is rooted, not in lust, but rather in unacknowledged negative feelings such as anxiety, loneliness and depression. The attraction to sexual arousal and satisfaction is a way of counteracting negative feelings by experiencing excitement and pleasure. But often it is followed by feelings of failure and shame, thereby adding to the initial negative feelings. It is, therefore, a typical example of a vicious circle.

- Using computers/the internet/mobile phones in an obsessive way. Social media addiction is a term that is often used to refer to someone who spends too much time on social media like Facebook and Twitter, or other forms of social media. As a result, it affects the person's daily life.

- Playing video games in a compulsive way.

- Workaholism. Instead of working to live, addicts of this kind live to work while neglecting their primary relationships, e.g. with their spouse and children.

- Exercising addiction. Some people get hooked on the opiate drugs that are naturally secreted in their brains by taking lots of exercise, e.g. running long distances.

- Spiritual obsession (as opposed to true religious devotion) which seeks security in the religion of God rather than the God of religion. It often adopts a rigid, legalistic, black and white, attitude.

- Pain addiction. Masochists who, for unconscious reasons, desire to suffer.
- Shopping addiction, when strictly speaking the person doesn't need anything in particular. Allied to that is the problem of kleptomania, i.e. compulsive stealing.
- Gambling in a compulsive way.

In all these and other such cases, a person uses a substance or behaviour in order to alter his or her negative mood. Gerald May, who refers to well over 100 addictions, suggests that the question is not, 'Do you have an addiction?' but, rather, 'What addictions do you have?' That said, it is true, of course, that some addictions, such as alcoholism and gambling, are more destructive than others, like eating chocolate. There is a sad paradox involved in all kinds of addiction. Inner pain drives many people to look for false forms of relief, and their resulting addictions reinforce rather than reduce their sufferings.

CHAPTER ELEVEN

PSYCHO-SPIRITUAL CAUSES *&* EFFECTS OF ADDICTION

Basically addictions, like alcoholism, are illnesses, which can have negative effects from a spiritual and moral point of view. We can look at two of these effects.

Firstly, Gerald May makes the interesting observation that addictions are what medieval spiritual writers used to refer to as 'bad habits' and 'attachments'. The English word 'attachment' is derived from the old French *atache,* meaning 'nailed to'. In other words, addictions nail down our spiritual desire for transcendent meaning, thereby cutting us off, to a greater or lesser extent, from a conscious experience of God.

While the desire of addicted people to experience happiness is healthy, the way in which they try to satisfy it is not. Unwittingly, it leads to idolatry by making created things such as alcohol, pills and work into substitutes for God. Understood in this objective sense, addictions are contrary to the first commandment which says, "You shall worship the Lord your God and him only shall you serve. You shall have no other gods before me" (Ex 20:3). As Jesus reminded us, "you cannot serve God and money [and by extension any worldly thing]" (Mt 6:24). In Phil 3:19, St Paul tells us that he wept for those whose "god is the belly" (gluttony is symbolic of excessive reliance on any created object).

Secondly, from an objective point of view, addictions such as alcoholism, drug taking and inappropriate sexual activity result in objectively grave sin. Talking about drinking alcohol to excess the Bible has a good deal to say. In Prov 23:29-35 we read: "Who has woe? Who has sorrow? Who has strife? Who has complaints? Who has needless bruises? Who has bloodshot eyes? Those who linger over wine, who go to sample bowls of mixed wine. Do not gaze at wine when it is red, when it sparkles in the cup, when it goes down smoothly! In the end it bites like a snake and poisons like a viper. Your eyes will see strange sights and your mind imagine confusing things." Scripture warns that heavy drinkers can act in an irreligious way: "Woe to those who rise early in the morning to run after their drinks, who stay up late at night till they are inflamed with wine. They... have no regard for the deeds of the Lord, no respect for the work of his hands" (Is 5:11-12). In Hab 2:15 it says that heavy drinking can lead to sexual impropriety. Ministerial effectiveness too, can be hampered by drunkenness, "Priests and prophets stagger from beer and are befuddled with wine; they reel from beer, they stagger when seeing visions, they stumble when rendering decisions" (Is 28:7-8). In Gal 5:21, St Paul says that drunkenness is sinful, and adds ominously, "I warn you as I warned you before; those who do such things will not inherit the kingdom of God!".

From a subjective point of view there is often diminished responsibility due to environmental, physical and unconscious influences which lessen the degree of consent. However, these pathological problems can be exploited by the Evil One. He can use them to seduce people into actions that cause serious harm both to themselves and to other people. For example, alcoholics and drug addicts can neglect their primary relationships, tell lies to get out of trouble, steal money to finance their excesses, endanger life by driving under the influence, give bad example to young people, and act in an irresponsible way, perhaps by getting involved in inappropriate sexual relationships. In many cities around the world, the rising tide of crime is due, in large part, to the increasing numbers of drug addicts who need vast sums of money to pay for their expensive substances. Working as a priest, I have found that many of the troubled people I deal with, are the children of addicted parents, especially of alcoholics and drug addicts. Almost invariably they have been badly affected by their negative experiences.

SOME PSYCHO-SPIRITUAL CAUSES OF ADDICTION

Bill Wilson, a co-founder of Alcoholics Anonymous was open-minded when it came to an understanding of the causes and cures of addiction. He wrote, "We welcome new and valuable knowledge whether it issues from a test tube, from a psychiatrist's couch, or from revealing social studies... we can accomplish together what we could never accomplish in separation and rivalry."[56] When one reads about the origins of AA it is clear that three psychologists in particular cast light on the subject of addiction.

Carl Jung argued that human maturity consisted of three things:
1. Accepting oneself with all of one's imperfections.
2. Being oneself, rather than wearing a mask and playing a part.
3. Forgetting oneself in outgoing love of others.

He felt that many people failed to mature because of a lack of self-acceptance. In his book, *Psychology and Western Religion,* he wrote these memorable words in a chapter entitled, "Psychotherapists or the Clergy"

> "Perhaps this sounds very simple, but simple things are always the most difficult. In real life it requires great discipline to be simple, and the acceptance of oneself is the key to the moral problem and of a whole outlook upon life. That I feed the hungry, forgive an insult and love my enemy in the name of Christ – all these are undoubtedly great virtues. After all, what I do for the least of my brothers and sisters, that I do to Christ. But what if I discover that the least among them all, the poorest of all the beggars, the worst of all the offenders, the very enemy himself – that these are within me, and that I stand in need of the handout of my own kindness – that I myself am the enemy who must be loved – what then?"[57]

------

56 Quoted in *As Bill Sees it (New York: Alcoholics Anonymous World Services, 167), 45.*
57 (London: Ark, 1988), 207.

The extent to which adults lack self-acceptance is the extent to which they will be neurotic. Carl Jung wrote:

"Neurosis is an inner division - the state of being at war with oneself. Everything that accentuates this division makes the person worse... What drives people to war with themselves is the suspicion that they consist of two persons in opposition to one another... Neurosis is a splitting of personality."[58]

While people can accept and love the aspects of their personalities that live up to their beliefs, ideals and values, they tend to reject and despise that part of their personalities which fails to do so. As a result, neurotic people tend to wear a mask and only reveal that part of themselves which they think will be acceptable and attractive to others. Meantime they conceal the weaker more vulnerable aspects of their personalities in a hypocritical sort of way. In Greek drama the term hypocrite was applied to an actor on the theatre stage who wore a mask and pretended to be someone other than him or herself. As a result, the word hypocrite was applied metaphorically to a person who "acts a part" in real life.

Lack of self-acceptance and inner conflict are like a toothache of the heart. If you have a pain in your jaw it will distract you from paying self-forgetful attention to other people. It is the same with unresolved emotional pain. Many people who lack self-acceptance suffer from excessive self-reference and seek consolation for their emotional conflicts by taking substances or engaging in activities that help them to escape from their inner suffering. It is like administering an anaesthetic. So, alcohol or hard drugs are taken in an attempt to deaden inner emotional distress. However, it often leads to the added suffering of shameful failure.

Jung was convinced that no neurotic ever recovered from his or her neurosis without having genuine religious experience. It is worth remembering that many of Jung's patients were practising

---

58   *Psychology and Western Religion*, op. cit., 208:

Christians, indeed some of them were clergymen. He argued that they got ill because, although they were committed to Christian doctrines and rituals, they were starved of conscious experience of God. He wrote, "The craving for alcohol is the equivalent, on a low level, of the spiritual thirst of our being for wholeness, expressed in medieval language: it is a desire for union with God."[59] To illustrate his meaning he quoted a verse of scripture: "As the deer longs for flowing streams, so my soul longs for you, O God" (Ps 42:1). In other words, when people seek ecstatic happiness and a sense of belonging by drinking alcohol, taking drugs etc., they are looking for the right thing, in the wrong place. Later in the same letter Jung made the perceptive observation, "You see, "alcohol" in Latin is "*spiritus*" and you use the same word for the highest religious experience (i.e. the Holy Spirit) as well as for the most depraving poison (i.e. alcoholic spirits). The helpful formula therefore is: *spiritus contra spiritum* (i.e. the Spirit versus spirits)."[60] Put another way, a person will overcome addiction to spirits such as whiskey and by extension any other addiction, if and when, he or she is filled with the Holy Spirit, i.e. the Higher Power.

William James also had interesting things to say about the causes and cures of addiction in his well-known book *Varieties of Religious Experience.* It argued in chapter four to seven that there are sick-souled, once born individuals and healthy-minded twice born people.

- People who are healthy-minded tend to have a very positive outlook on life, they see everything as good, while being inclined to minimise the reality of evil. They have sunny, enthusiastic temperaments and, from a religious point of view, they have a spirit of grateful admiration and a desire for union with the divine. James cites Walt Whitman, the American poet, as an example of this kind of outlook.
- Sick-souled people, on the other hand, are painfully aware of

---

59   Letter of Bill Wilson to Carl Jung, Jan 23rd 1961. It is mentioned in the *Big Book* (New York: Alcoholics World Services, 2001), 26-27.

60   Ibid.

evil in the world. They tend to be melancholic and fearful. They acknowledge that the evil they sense in outer reality resonates within their own minds as well. No matter how neurotic they may be, sick-souled people encompass this broader range of experience. James cited Leo Tolstoy, a Russian novelist, as an example of this type. He felt that sick-souled people were more likely to become addicted, e.g. to alcohol.

Religious conversion enables sick-souled people, in particular, to experience inner healing as a result of a reconciliation between the Dr Jeckel (positive) and Mr Hyde (negative) sides of their personalities. James described the dynamic in these words: "To be converted is the process, gradual or sudden, by which a self hitherto divided, and consciously wrong, inferior and unhappy, becomes unified and consciously right, superior and happy, in consequence of its firmer hold upon religious realities."[61] In another place he wrote, "The sway of alcohol over mankind is unquestionably due to its power to stimulate the mystical faculties of human nature, usually crushed to earth by the cold facts and dry criticisms of the sober hour... The drunken consciousness is one bit of the mystic consciousness."[62] James stressed the role of the unconscious in all this. Things happen in the mind of the troubled person that he or she is not fully aware of. There is a kind of incubation period when the unconscious prepares the person for a sudden shift in consciousness. These forces often transcend the individual, i.e. by means of the unmerited experience of a Higher Power.

Viktor Frankl was born in Austria. He went through an atheistic phase in his teenage years. Although there was a religious dimension to all his adult writings he was reluctant to say whether he was a believer or not. He explained, "I do not allow myself to confess personally whether I'm religious or not. I'm writing as a psychologist, I'm writing as a psychiatrist, I'm writing as a man of the med-

---

61   *Varieties of Religious Experience* (London: Fontana, 1971), 104.
62   *Varieties of Religious Experience,* op. cit., 373.

ical faculty... And that makes the message more powerful because if you were identifiably religious, immediately people would say, 'Oh well, he's that religious psychologist.'[63] Frankl believed that human beings were naturally spiritual. He defined spirituality as a desire or search for unconditional meaning. Our deepest desire, he maintained, is not for happiness, power, pleasure, self-realisation, self-fulfilment, self-development or self-actualisation. It is through the self-transcending pursuit of meaning that these other desirable states can follow.

Frankl believed that in modern secular culture many people are starved of the meanings he had discussed. That absence leads them to suffer from an emptiness at the centre of their lives, what he called "existential frustration" which often finds expression in boredom and angst. Interestingly, he said that it gave rise to Sunday neurosis, "the kind of depression which afflicts people who become aware of the lack of content in their lives when the rush of the busy week is over and the void within them becomes manifest."[64] Frankl believed that existential frustration was the bitter fruit of a constricted, underdeveloped human spirit which was starved of the oxygen of meaning. He wrote, "this existential vacuum, along with other causes, can result in neurotic illness."[65] Frankl also believed that when people suppressed their religious sense, their unfulfilled desire for meaning would be displaced into unhealthy attitudes and behaviours. They would end up making things like addictions more likely.

Frankl believed that common problems in Western countries, such as addiction, were often rooted in the experience of existential frustration. He explained:

....

63 Matthew Scully, "Viktor Frankl at Ninety: An Interview," *First Things* (April 1995).

64 *Man's Search for Meaning* (New York: Pocket Books, 1963), 169.

65 *Psychology and Existentialism: Selected Papers on Logotherapy* (London: Penguin Books, 1967), 50.

"Sometimes the frustrated will to meaning is vicariously compensated for by a will to power, including the most primitive form of the will to power, the will to money. In other cases, the place of the frustrated will to meaning is taken by the will to pleasure. That is why existential frustration often leads to sexual compensation. We can observe in such cases that the sexual libido becomes rampant in the existential vacuum."[66]

Frankl believed that a person would only recover from such things as neurosis and addictions of different kinds by discovering a sense of unconditional meaning in life. In his *Recollections: An Autobiography*, he admitted that the phrase "unconditional meaning" was a way of referring to the higher power or God.

The goal of American psychologist Abraham Maslow was to integrate into a single theoretical structure the partial truths he saw in the writings of colleagues such as Freud, Adler and Jung. He felt that whereas Sigmund Freud supplied psychologists with the sick half of psychology, he focused on the healthy half. Instead of studying neurotics as Freud and Jung had done, Maslow decided to study people who were very successful at living – he called them self-actualisers – in order to see what made them tick.

Maslow found that people were motivated by a succession of hierarchically ordered needs:

1. Physiological needs such as food, drink, oxygen, rest, activity and sex.
2. Safety needs such as protection from dangerous people, objects and situations in the form of things like the weather, illness etc.
3. Love and belongingness needs, such as a sense of affection, acceptance and identification with a group/s.
4. Esteem needs in the form of competence at what one is doing and having the respect and goodwill of others.

66 *Man's Search for Meaning,* op. cit., 170.

5. Cognitive needs for knowledge and understanding, an ability to satisfy one's curiosity in such a way as to make sense of things.
6. Aesthetic needs such as beauty in art, symmetry in nature, balance, order and form in all things.
7. Self-actualisation needs i.e. fulfilling one's full potential, everything one is capable of becoming.

Although Maslow himself was an atheist, he found that self-actualised people often reported having what he called peak-experiences and he found that, by and large, such experiences were religious in nature. He cited Marghanita Laski's book *Ecstasy*[67] because it contained many examples of the theistic and non-theistic spiritual experiences he had in mind. These epiphanies were triggered by such things as scenes of natural beauty, religious rituals, creative activity, scientific discovery, intellectual insight, sexual experience, childbirth etc. Maslow himself testified to the fact that he had enjoyed such experiences. For instance, speaking about a visit to Boston he said:

"The first time I saw the Charles river I almost died... It was a very, very great experience, profoundly aesthetic... I remember collapsing in a chair and looking at all this in just perfect wonder... The place was so beautiful that it would crack your skull open, it was almost painful."[68]

Like Jung and Frankl, Maslow believed that genuine religious experiences, of the kind he described, could have a therapeutic effect. He wrote:

"The power of the peak-experience could permanently affect one's attitude toward life. A single glimpse of heaven is enough to confirm its existence even if it is never experienced

67 *Ecstasy in Secular and Religious Experience* (London: Cresset Press, 1965).
68 Edward Hoffman, *The Right to be Human: A Biography of Abraham Maslow* (Northhamptonshire: Crucible, 1989), 267.

again. It is my strong suspicion that one such experience might be able to prevent suicide, for instance, and perhaps, many varieties of low self-destruction, such as alcoholism, drug addiction and addiction to violence."[69]

69   *The Right to be Human: A Biography of Abraham Maslow*, op. cit., 277.

CHAPTER TWELVE

ORIGINS OF AA & 12 STEP PROGRAMMES

On one occasion Jung treated an American alcoholic, called Rowland Hazard for a year, ultimately without success. Then the addicted man asked him whether he could give him any reason for hope. Jung replied, "There is one more resource and that is a conversion experience. I know you are already a man of faith and of belief, but I am talking about a transforming experience." "Well," said Rowland, "Where do I find such a thing?" The doctor responded, "those things just happen. The lightning strikes some people; and not others." In the event Hazard had such a liberating religious experience as a result of attending an evangelical meeting run by the Oxford Group. Its teachings rested on to be spiritually reborn, the Oxford Group advocated Six Steps:

1. A complete deflation
2. Dependence on God
3. A moral inventory
4. Confession
5. Restitution
6. Continued work with others in need

When Hazard returned from Switzerland he helped a friend of his, Edwin Thatcher to recover from alcoholism when he too had a profound experience of God. Thatcher had a friend, Bill Wilson, a stockbroker who was a chronic alcoholic.

Wilson had a very difficult childhood. His father deserted his mother, his sister and himself. Soon afterwards Bill's mother got a divorce. Then she went away to study so Bill was left with her parents. In secondary school he fell in love with a girl named Bertha but she died suddenly. Bill was plunged into depression and failed to graduate with his class. He recalled, "I was unable to finish because I could not accept the loss of any part of what I thought *belonged* to me."

At the age of 22 he attended a party where he felt awkward and socially inept. Then someone gave him his first drink. He wrote:

> "My self-consciousness was such that I simply had to take that drink. So, I took it, and another one, then another. That strange barrier that existed between me and all men and women seemed to instantly go down. I felt that I belonged where I was, belonged to life, I belonged to the universe, I was part of things at last."[70]

Clearly, Bill Wilson craved a sense of belonging, but in his early life the only way he could experience it was by overcoming his inhibitions by means of drinking to excess. Not surprisingly, Bill soon became a chronic alcoholic. Instead of bringing him a sense of lasting happiness, excessive drinking, like any addiction, compounded his problems and increased his sense of misery and isolation. Some years later Wilson recounted,

> "Hearing of my plight, my friend Edwin Thatcher came to see me at my home where I was drinking. By then, it was November 1934, I had long marked my friend Edwin for a hopeless case. Yet there he was in a very evident state of 'release' which could by no means be accounted for by his mere association, for a very short time, with the Oxford Groups. Yet this obvious state of release, as distinct from his usual depression, was tremendously convincing. Because he was a kindred sufferer, he could unquestionably communicate with me at great depth. I knew at once I must find an experience like his, or die."[71]

---

70   *Pass It On* (New York: Alcoholics Anonymous World Services, 1984), 56.
71   Letter of Bill Wilson to Carl Jung, Jan 23rd 1961. It is mentioned in the *Big Book* (New York: Alcoholics World Services, 2001), 26-27.

Sometime later while he was in hospital Wilson cried out in utter despair, "If there be a God, will He show Himself." This desperate desire was fulfilled when he had a quasi-mystical experience. He described it in these vivid words,

"Suddenly, my room blazed with an indescribable white light. I was seized with an ecstasy beyond description... Then, seen in the mind's eye, there was a mountain. I stood upon its summit, where a great wind blew. A wind, not of air, but of spirit. In great, clean strength, it blew right through me. Then came the blazing thought, 'You are a free man.' ... a great peace stole over me... I became acutely conscious of a Presence which seemed like a veritable sea of living spirit... 'This,' I thought, 'must be the great reality. The God of the preachers.' I seemed to be possessed by the absolute, and the curious conviction deepened that no matter how wrong things seemed to be, there could be no question of the ultimate rightness of God's universe. For the first time I felt that I really belonged. I knew I was loved and could love in return."[72]

Afterwards Wilson wrote,

"Defective relations with other human beings have nearly always been the immediate cause of our woes, including our alcoholism... Salvation in AA consisted in emerging from isolation to the feeling of being at one with God and man. To the sense of belonging that comes to us. We no longer live in a completely hostile world. We are no longer lost and frightened and purposeless."[73]

Bill Wilson was 39 when he had that vivid religious experience. He

---

72 Bill Wilson, *Alcoholics Anonymous Comes of Age* (New York: Alcoholics Anonymous World Services, 1979), 121.

73 Ernest Kurtz, *Not-God: A History of Alcoholics Anonymous* (Center City, MN: Hazelden, 1991), 125.

never drank again. But soon afterwards he was tempted to do so when he was away from home in a hotel feeling lonely. Instead of taking a drink, however, he telephoned the director of a local church who told him about an alcoholic called Dr Bob Smith. Bill Wilson called to see him. That was the first ever A.A. meeting. They had discovered an important key to recovery. In giving one receives (cf. Lk 6:38; Acts 20:35). One holds on to one's own sobriety by helping another alcoholic to either attain or maintain his or her sobriety. Evidently, when two people share the same struggle they provide one another with a sense of belonging as they help one another to get well.

In the wake of his dramatic conversion Bill Wilson conceived the idea of a society of alcoholics, where each member would transmit his or her experience to the next. If each sufferer were to point out to prospective new members, the hopelessness of alcoholism from a scientific point of view, he or she might be able to alert the newcomers to the need to be open to an equally transforming spiritual experience. This concept proved to be the foundation of the success of Alcoholics Anonymous. The famous, twelve steps, which owed a lot to the disciplines of the Oxford Group, were formulated by Bill Wilson, with Dr Bob Smith's help. Later Bill Wilson was mainly responsible for writing what is known affectionately as The Big Book, *Alcoholics Anonymous: The Story of How Many Thousands of Men and Women Have Recovered from Alcoholism*. It contains an enormous amount of practical wisdom about the meaning and implications of the twelve steps.

It is worth noting that some 27 years after attaining his sobriety, Wilson wrote a very interesting letter to Carl Jung in mid January 1961. As well as telling the famous doctor about his addiction and recovery he said:

"I doubt if you are aware that a certain conversation you once had with one of your patients, a Mr Rowland Hazard, back in the early 1930's, played a critical role in the founding of our Fellowship."

Wilson went on to add,

"Very many thoughtful members of A.A. are students of your writings. Because of your conviction that man is something more than intellect, emotion, and two dollars worth of chemicals, you have especially endeared yourself to us."[74]

74 *Big Book*, op. cit., 26-27.

CHAPTER THIRTEEN

OVERCOMING ADDICTION

We know from experience, that if we wish to overcome our addictions, it is a notoriously difficult thing to do. Before suggesting how we might go about the task, I'd like to mention an approach that does not work. Clearly, many, if not most addictions, are the result of inner hurts, e.g. Bill Wilson and his sister were abandoned by their father and mother in childhood. As a result, they limped out of childhood with many inner hurts. Some addicts try to deal with the emotional causes of their excesses, by getting involved in counselling and different forms of therapy. Normally, they don't work. A few years ago, a member of AA informed me why this was so. He had set up a clinic which helped alcoholics to give up drinking. He said, "Many of them want therapy in order to get off the booze. But, I tell them that until they come off the drink, therapy will not help them." I have noticed that psychiatrist Gerald May shares that opinion. In a book entitled *Care of Mind, Care of Spirit* he wrote, "Attempts to stop dependency through psychotherapy or self-understanding seldom work. Such endeavours have put the cart before the horse. The pattern of chemical abuse must be broken first; then psychotherapy may be in order."[75]

When Bill Wilson and Dr Bob overcame their addiction to alcohol, the former wrote what are known as the 12 steps to sobriety. I will mention what the steps are and then go on to comment on them.

1. We admitted we were powerless over alcohol - that our lives had become unmanageable.
2. Came to believe that a power greater than ourselves could restore us to sanity.

75 *Care of Mind/Care of Spirit: A Psychiatrist Explores Spiritual Direction* (San Francisco: Harper, 1982), 132.

3. Made a decision to turn our will and our lives over to the care of God as we understood Him.

4. Made a searching and fearless moral inventory of ourselves.

5. Admitted to God, to ourselves, and to another human being the exact nature of our wrongs.

6. Were entirely ready to have God remove all these defects of character.

7. Humbly asked Him to remove our shortcomings.

8. Made a list of all persons we had harmed, and became willing to make amends to them all.

9. Made direct amends to such people wherever possible, except when to do so would injure them or others.

10. Continued to take personal inventory and when we were wrong, promptly admitted it.

11. Sought through prayer and meditation to improve our conscious contact with God as we understood Him, praying only for knowledge of His will for us and the power to carry that out.

12. Having had a spiritual awakening as the result of these steps, we tried to carry this message to alcoholics and to practice these principles in all our affairs.

While these steps were originally intended to help alcoholics to recover, they have been adapted since then, so that people suffering from any kind of addiction can use them to great effect. Nowadays they are used by over a hundred recovery groups of different kinds. It is arguable, that the 12 steps constitute one of the most significant American contributions to spirituality in the 20th Century. Fr Ed Dowling, Bill Wilson's Jesuit sponsor, pointed out that there were a number of similarities between the Twelve Steps and *The Spiritual Exercises* of St Ignatius of Loyola, which Bill read with great interest. Dr Bob Smith revealed, in one of his talks, that the principal ideas that influenced the spirituality of the A.A. in the early days, came from the Bible, mainly 1 Corinthians 13, the Sermon on the Mount in Matthew, and the letter of James, whose practical approach was so influential that some early members wanted to call the A.A. fellowship "the James Club". The meetings held in Dr Bob's hometown of Akron, Ohio, between 1935 and 1939, were associated with the Oxford Group. The pioneers of that time went so far as to call themselves the "Alcoholic Squad of the Oxford Group". During the period when members were in recovery, they usually had a quiet time each morning. It involved Bible study, prayer to God, listening for messages from God, and the use of helpful meditation literature. There were frequent discussions of every-day problems in the light of Biblical teaching.

It is worth mentioning that Bill Wilson's long-suffering wife Lois started a group for the wives and dependants of recovering alcoholics which eventually evolved into what is known as Al-Anon. There is a movie entitled, *When Love is not Enough: The Lois Wilson Story* (2010). There is also a movie about Bill Wilson's life entitled, *My Name is Bill W* (1989). One can also view a very interesting interview on Youtube entitled, *Bill and Lois Tell their Story*.

DEVELOPMENT OF THE CAME TO BELIEVE RETREATS

Clarence Snyder was another of the founding members of A.A. Together with Dr Bob Smith it was he who built on the spiritual foundations of the fellowship by developing the Came to Believe Retreats. They were designed to foster absolute honesty, purity, unselfishness and love in the members. He believed that the steps could be grouped as follows

- Step one: Admission
- Steps two to seven: Submission (where those in recovery submit their lives and wills to God's care)
- Steps eight to nine: Restitution
- Steps ten to twelve: Construction and maintenance.

Here are scripture texts that can accompany the 12 steps.
1. "I know that nothing good lives in me, that is, in my sinful nature. For I have the desire to do what is good, but I cannot carry it out." (Romans 7:18)
2. "My grace is sufficient for you, for my POWER is made

perfect in weakness." (2 Cor 12:9) "...for it is God Who works in you to will and act according to His good purpose." (Phil. 2:13)

3. "If anyone would come after me, he must deny himself and take up his cross daily and follow me." (Lk 9:23)

4. "Let us examine our ways and test them, and let us return to the Lord." (Lam 3:40)

5. "Therefore confess your sins to each other and pray for each other so that you may be healed." (Jm 5:16)

6. "If you are willing and obedient, you will eat the best from the land." (Is 1:19)

7. "Humble yourselves before the Lord, and He will lift you up." (Jm 4:10)

8. "Therefore, if you are offering your gift at the altar and there remember that your brother has something against you, leave your gift there in front of the altar. First go and be reconciled to your brother; then come and offer your gift." (Mt 5:23, 24)

9. "Give and it shall be given you. A good measure, pressed down, shaken together and running over, will be poured into your lap. For with the measure you use, it will be measured to you." (Lk 6:38)

10. "For by the grace given me I say to every one of you: Do not think of yourself more highly than you ought, but rather think of yourself with sober judgment, in accordance with the measure of faith GOD has given you." (Rm 12:3)

11. "May the words of my mouth and the meditation of my heart be pleasing in your sight, O Lord, my Rock and my Redeemer." (Ps 19:14). "Let the word of Christ dwell in you richly..." (Col. 3:16)

12. "Brothers, if someone is caught in a sin, you who are spiritual should restore him gently. But watch yourself, or you also may be tempted. Carry each other's burdens, and in this way you will fulfill the Law of Christ." (Gal 6:1-2).

At this point I am going to presume to offer some personal reflection on the 12 steps. For a fuller treatment written by recovering alcoholics see Clarence Snyder's helpful, *Our A.A. Legacy to the Faith Community.*

CHAPTER FOURTEEN

BREAKING FREE: STEPS ONE TO FIVE

STEP ONE

Firstly, people who want to recover from an addiction need to notice and admit that they are addicted. Relatives, friends and colleagues are often painfully aware of the fact, while the addict goes on denying reality. "I know I drink," says an alcoholic, "but I'm in control, I could stop any time. After all, last year I was off the booze for the whole of Lent." Admittedly, it is easier to acknowledge a chocolate or caffeine addiction than to own up to alcohol or sex addiction. It has probably to do with the degree of dependency, social stigma and shame involved. That is why the first of the Twelve Steps to recovery begins by saying: "We admitted that we were powerless over (whatever form of addiction afflicts us) and that our lives had become unmanageable."

STEP TWO

Secondly, addicts need to move from *desiring* to give up an addiction, to *wanting* to do so. As a result of smoking heavily for years, I quickly became addicted to nicotine. I not only admitted that I was hooked, I also recognised that the practice was bad for my health. So, on many occasions, I resolved to kick the habit. Like many other smokers, I did so, time and time again. In 1982-3, I was living in the chaplain's quarters of an American hospital. To get to my room I had to go through a ward on the third floor. It was full of men and women suffering from chest complaints, many of which had been caused by smoking. When I'd hear them coughing, wheezing and gasping for breath, I'd think, "If I don't give up the cigarettes, I could end up in a ward like this." I decided to make yet another effort to stop smoking. But on this occasion there was something new. It was the difference between wishing and willing. Whereas in the past I had *desired* to give up, on this occasion I really *wanted* to do so. At five minutes to midnight on Shrove Tuesday 1983, I smoked my last cigarette and, with the help of God, I have never taken a puff since then.

Reliance on God as one understands God is absolutely vital. Not every addicted person will have a clear sense of who God is or what God is like. The greater power could be seen as a Creative intelligence, or a Spirit of the Universe underlying the totality of things. James Fowler used to talk about a centre of Power and Value beyond one's everyday self.[76] For many Christians, the higher power will be synonymous with the God of the New Testament, Father, Son and Holy Spirit.

STEP THREE

Thirdly, addicted people need to admit that they are powerless over their addictions. Instead of controlling the addiction, they are controlled by it. This is a vital realisation, because it enables the wilful ego to give up its illusion of control and to open up to the Higher Power which works in and through the neglected and constricted, deeper self (cf. Eph 3:16). To help me to appreciate the implications of that point, I sometimes engage in what I refer to as my Holy Saturday meditation. I imagine that I approach the tomb of Jesus and ease myself past the stone at the entrance. When I get inside the burial place I find that it is very dark. But after a while my eyes get accustomed to the gloom and I can dimly see the embalmed body of Jesus lying on a shelf of rock. I go over and lie down beside him because there is enough room to do so. I turn on my side and look at the bloodstained outline of his body beneath the burial cloths. I ask myself, "who is this lying beside me?" I am amazed as I find myself replying, "this is Jesus Christ, the Son of God, and here he is lying beside me devoid of breath, pulse or life. The all powerful One has become utterly powerless." Then I say to the inanimate corpse of Jesus, "I experience lots of weakness in different areas of my life such as overcoming such

---

76 James Fowler, *Stages of Faith: The Psychology of Human Development and the Quest for Meaning* (San Francisco: Harper & Row, 1981), 23.

and such addiction." Sometime later, I imagine that I see a blazing light illumine the tomb. I know that it is the light of the Holy Spirit. It invades the lifeless body of Jesus and raises it to glorious and everlasting, new life. As he ascends, I cry out to him and say, "Lord Jesus don't forget about me, I need to experience the same power of the Holy Spirit in the powerlessness of my addiction."

St Paul experienced this truth in his own life. When he asked the Lord on three occasions to remove a metaphorical thorn, of an unknown nature, from his flesh,[77] God replied, "My grace is sufficient for you, for my power is made perfect in weakness" (2 Cor 12:9). Paul endorsed the truth of that promise when he said, "I can do everything through him who gives me strength" (Phil 4:13). These important points are relevant in every aspect of daily Christian living, especially in the struggle against addiction. Once we hear the voice of the Lord, the Spirit will not only enable us to want to do God's will, no matter how difficult it might seem, it will also give us the power to do so. As 1 Peter 4:11 urged, "If anyone serves, he should do it *with the strength God provides*, so that in all things God may be praised through Jesus Christ." In Eph 1:19-20, Paul says that the power the believer receives is, "the same mighty power that raised Christ from the dead."

This is Dr Bob's Third Step Prayer. "Dear God, I'm sorry about the mess I've made of my life. I want to turn away from all the wrong things I've ever done and all the wrong things I've ever been. Please forgive me for it all. I know you have the power to change my life and can turn me into a winner. Thank You, God for getting my attention long enough to interest me in trying it your way. God, please take over the management of my life and everything about me. I am making this conscious decision to turn my will and my life over to your care and am asking you to please take over all parts of my life. Please, God, move into my heart. However you do it is your business, but make Yourself real inside me and fill my awful emptiness. Fill me with Your love and Holy Spirit and make me know Your will for me. And now, God, help Yourself to me and keep on doing it. I'm not sure I want You

---

77   It was an unknown malady such as epilepsy or short sightedness.

to, but do it anyhow. I rejoice that I am now a part of Your people, that my uncertainty is gone forever and that You now have control of my will and my life. Thank You and I praise Your name. Amen."

Steps four to five

Steps 4 and 5 of AA state, "Made a searching and fearless moral inventory of ourselves. Admitted to God, to ourselves, and to another human being the exact nature of our wrongs." Clarence Snyder said, "This is the misunderstood step. We are talking about the 'nature' of our wrongs – not necessarily all the details of each act we have done."[78] Presumably what he is getting at is the fact that it's the attitudes that underlie bad acts that are important to notice such as pride, resentment, envy etc. Karl Rogers, one of the founders of modern counselling practice believed that if lack of self-acceptance is the basic human problem, what addicts need from counsellors, and by extension from friends and confidants, is unconditional, non-judgemental acceptance and love. Bill Wilson, author of the 12 steps of Alcoholics Anonymous, realised this. Therefore, these two steps enable the recovering person to move from being merely dry, to enjoying genuine sobriety. This is so, because they have tackled the problem of a lack of self-acceptance which is one of the main underlying causes of addiction.

It is important that recovering addicts make a fearless, conscientious moral inventory of their past wrongs without trying to excuse or blame others for them. There is a prayer that can be said at a time like this. "May the Lord who enlightens every heart, enlighten mine to acknowledge my wrongdoings while trusting in God's mercy." I know that some people in recovery look at their lives in ten-year segments, from their childhood up to their present age. It is a good thing to write down the results on a sheet/s of paper.

When recovering alcoholics have asked me to accompany them as they made step five, I witnessed their inner healing occurring. That step requires people to have a heartfelt desire to take off their

---

78   *Our A.A. Legacy to the Faith Community,* op. cit., 29.

customary masks and to be their true, vulnerable selves. As this desire strengthens, it begins to override a deep-seated fear of rejection which usually echoes back to childhood. As recovering addicts begin to lower their defences and to courageously tell their confidant about the darker side of their natures while sensing the understanding and acceptance of the listener, a wonderful reconciliation begins to take place. In the light of this empathic understanding, they begin to understand, accept, and love themselves as they are, and not as they have pretended to be. I'm sure that such acceptance, in the light of another person's love, mediates the healing love of a merciful God. As St James once wrote: "Confess your sins to one another, and pray for one another that you may be healed" (Jm 5:16). As a result, the dividing wall between the acceptable and the unacceptable self begins to break down (cf. Eph 2:14), and the recovering addict is strengthened in his or her innermost self by the Spirit (cf. Eph 3:16). At this point the person in recovery goes beyond being dry to become truly sober. This is so because, as we have already noted, the underlying cause of his or her addiction, namely self-rejection, has begun to be dealt with. People who have completed step five can begin to say this prayer in a heartfelt way.

"Lord, help me to go on facing the truth about myself no matter how beautiful it may be. Enable me, to see and to love in others, especially the poor, needy, and addicted the inner glory you are already seeing and loving in me. Amen."

CHAPTER FIFTEEN

HEALING *&* RECONCILIATION: STEPS SIX TO NINE

STEP SIX

While addicted people in recovery acknowledge that environmental and unconscious factors contributed to their addiction, they themselves had a free and conscious role to play. Defects of character such as pride, excessive self-reference and self-indulgence contributed to their troubles. So not surprisingly, step six says that the person in recovery needs to be entirely ready to have God remove all these defects of character. In this regard I'm reminded of something that Thomas à Kempis (1380-1471) said in chapter eleven of *The Imitation of Christ,* "if every year we uprooted a single fault, we would soon become perfect".

STEP SEVEN

To overcome defects of character, one has to discover the root of that defect. For example, like many alcoholics, Bill Wilson was prone to depression. It afflicted him a number of times during his life. Not surprisingly, he tried to understand its causes and to overcome it. While it could have had physical origins such as a lack of serotonin in his brain, Wilson said in a letter to a fellow sufferer, "I suppose about half the old-timers have neurotic hangovers of one sort or another. Certainly I can number myself among them." To overcome neuroses is not possible without divine help, so step seven suggests that the recovering addict should humbly ask the Lord's help, like any other believer, in order to remove his or her shortcomings. Bill Wilson found that Karen Horney's book *Neurosis and Human Growth* was very helpful in aiding him to understand his shortcomings and their origins. Speaking about its author, Wilson wrote: "I have the highest admiration for her. That gal's insights have been most helpful to me."

Horney argued that neurotic attitudes could be traced back to a lack of warmth and affection from parents in childhood, often because they were inhibited by neurotic problems of their own. Horney described some of the harmful things that parents do either intentionally or unintentionally. She pointed out that they engage in, "preference for other children, unjust reproaches, unpredictable changes between overindulgence and scornful rejection, unfulfilled promises, and not least important, an attitude towards the child's needs which goes through all gradations from temporary in-consideration to a consistent interfering with the most legitimate wishes of the child, such as disturbing friendships, ridiculing independent thinking, spoiling its interest in its own pursuits... direct or indirect domination, indifference, erratic behaviour, lack of respect for the child's individual needs, lack of real guidance, disparaging attitudes, too much admiration or the absence of it, lack of reliable warmth, having to take sides in parental disagreements, too much or too little responsibility, over-protection, isolation from other children, injustice, discrimination, un-kept promises, hostile atmosphere, and so on and so on."[79] Inadequate caring of this kind in childhood, alienates young people from their true selves while prompting a deep-seated sense of anxiety and hidden anger toward the powerful but indifferent adults. As a result, neurotic people subsequently spend an inordinate amount of time trying to cope with their anxiety and anger. Typically, they do this by avoiding, attacking, or completely complying with others. These three attitudes could be described as follows.

1. A compliant, self-effacing attitude says implicitly, "If you love me, you will not hurt me."
2. An aggressive, expansive attitude says implicitly, "If I have power, no one can hurt me."
3. A withdrawn, resigned attitude says implicitly, "If I withdraw, nothing can hurt me."

....

79 Karen Horney, *Our Inner Conflicts* vol. 2 (New York: Norton, 1945), 41.

Wilson was particularly impressed by the fact that Horney's book indicated that neurotic people were often motivated by an unhealthy drive for glory and a morbid sense of dependency. The search for glory is a drive that leads to an idealised self-image and a tendency to over-look neurotic conflicts. This compulsive, indiscriminate, insatiable urge to express the idealised self is also accompanied by the need for per-fection, neurotic ambition, and vindictive triumph. Like any neurotic drive, it causes intense anxiety when frustrated. One of its results is neurotic pride, the mood felt when one lives up to the "musts," "should," "oughts," and "have tos" of the idealised self. The elder brother in the parable of the Prodigal Son, epitomised this attitude.

The phrase morbid dependency refers to a neurotic need to feel part of something larger and more powerful than oneself. This need often manifests itself as excessive, compulsive religious devotion, identification with a group or cause, or morbid dependency in a lov-ing relationship. Love appears as the ticket to paradise, where all woes will end. There will be no more feelings of being lost, guilty, and unworthy; no more responsibility for self; no more struggle with a harsh world for which one feels "hopelessly unequipped".

In 1958 Wilson published an article entitled, "The Next Frontier: Emotional Sobriety" in *The Grapevine* magazine. It was quite clear that it had been influenced by Horney's writings. He said: "I kept ask-ing myself, "Why can't the Twelve Steps work to release my depres-sion?" He went on to answer: "Suddenly, I realised what the matter was. My basic flaw had always been dependence – almost absolute dependence – on people or circumstances to supply me with prestige, security and the like. Failing to get these things according to my per-fectionist dreams and specifications, I had fought for them. And when defeat came, so did my depression." In a way Bill Wilson's depression proved to be a blessing in disguise, in the sense that it forced him to acknowledge his inordinate attachments. Whereas psychology had provided the insight, his prayerful spirituality and reliance on God's grace helped him to overcome his neuroses, and hence his depres-sion. He wrote: "I could not avail myself of God's love until I was able to offer it back to Him by loving others as He would have me. And I couldn't possibly do that so long as I was victimised by false dependencies."

Here is a prayer, sometimes referred to as the miracle prayer, that can be said in conjunction with the foregoing steps.

"Dear God, I come to you in the name of Jesus. Thank you for taking complete control of my life in step three and thank you for this opportunity to wipe my slate clean and start my life over anew. I am coming to you on my knees in all humility to humbly ask you to forgive all my past wrongs and remove all my shortcomings.

I acknowledge that my past was sinful, and I ask you now, God to please forgive all my past sins. I am so thankful that you have promised to do this and that you have the power to do it if I but ask. I want to start a new life today, and I ask you to help me to do so and to keep helping if I keep asking.

In step three I turned my will and my life over to your care. In step four, five and six, I have completed my moral inventory and admitted to myself and another person the exact nature of my wrongs. I now admit these wrongs to you, Lord, and I am entirely ready to have you remove all my defects of character.

I am entirely ready and ask and pray that you remove from me every single defect of character listed in my fourth step moral inventory. Thank you, God, for help to remove all my defects of character. Please help me learn how to keep them out of my life through the effectiveness of step ten.

Thank you God, for this opportunity for a new beginning in my life and a chance to be a part of the solutions in life instead of the problems. Please grant me wisdom, knowledge, and strength as I go from here to do your work and live the victorious life you want for me. Thank you Jesus, for these twelve steps which will make your plan for my life clear to me. Thank you, and praise to your name. Amen."

STEP EIGHT

At this point the person in recovery makes a list of all the people they have harmed. The list would include people like the following:

- Parents, spouse, children, aunts, uncles, grandparents, neighbours, employers, employees, school friends, creditors, members of the opposite sex, childhood friends, teachers, business associates, people with whom you might have caused trouble or from whom you have stolen
- Anyone about whom you get an uncomfortable feeling when you think of them
- There were probably people that came to your mind as you were doing the fourth step.

A] BEING FORGIVEN

Many recovering addicts are weighed down by guilt on account of the immoral things they have done and the good deeds they have failed to do, especially when they were addicted. They need to accept that if they look into the eyes of God's mercy expecting only mercy they will receive only mercy. As St Paul said in Eph 2:8-10, "For it is by grace you have been saved, through faith — and this not from yourselves, it is the gift of God — not by works, so that no one can boast." This forgiveness is not something they earn or merit. It is the free gift of God.

B] FORGIVING OTHERS

While God's unconditional mercy is always available to us, we can only experience it in the depths of our hearts if we are willing to extend the same unconditional mercy to those who have hurt or offended us. There is a need for recovering addicts to consciously acknowledge the hurts and injustices they have experienced. Also, there is often a need to pray for the grace to remember repressed memories of hurt, injustice or deprivation, e.g. "Lord you know me through and through, if there is anyone you want me to forgive, help me to remember repressed memories and their associated negative feelings." Then when the time is right go on to forgive by saying a prayer like the following:

> "Lord Jesus I thank you for forgiving all my sins even though I didn't deserve to be forgiven. You have brought to mind those who have sinned against me in the past, and who caused me a good deal of hurt. Help me, by your grace to forgive. I know that in asking for this grace I am already receiving it because I am praying within the centrality of your will. In the name Jesus I now forgive you (name the person/s you have in mind) from my heart for the pain you caused me. I do so without judgement or condemnation. I release you, I call down God's blessing upon you and I thank God you are now forgiven. Amen."

C] ASKING FOR FORGIVENESS

Jesus wants people in recovery to break free of the gravitational pull of self-absorption in order to see things from other people's point of view. With God's help we need to become aware of the times we have hurt or injured others by deed or omission as a result of our addictions. Then we need to listen to the advice of Jesus, "if you are offering your gift at the altar and there remember that your brother has something against you, leave your gift there in front of the altar. First go and be reconciled to your brother; then come and offer your gift" (Mt 5:23-24). The Lord is clearly saying that reconciliation with the person who has something against us must take precedence over attendance at the Eucharist. We dare not come before God in the liturgy, or for that matter on judgment day, unless we are first reconciled with those we have hurt, injured or failed in any way.

You can apologise and seek forgiveness either in spoken words or by means of a well-thought-out letter or email. There is a right and a wrong way of doing this. When the wrong approach is used, there is an avoidance of personal responsibility. The addicted person who has hurt or injured another man, woman or child might say, "I'm sorry that you feel hurt." When the correct approach is adopted, you accept responsibility for what you did by saying, "I am sorry that I hurt you, it was my fault, and in humility I ask you for the gift of your forgiveness, which strictly speaking I don't deserve." It takes humility and courage to do this, because the other person might need time to forgive or might even refuse to forgive you. But although this is unfortunate, at least you have done your best to be reconciled. As St Paul says in Rom 12:18-19, "If it is possible, as far *as it depends on you*, live at peace with everyone."

STEP NINE

If you can make amends for what you have done, promise to do so, e.g. by giving back money you may have stolen, or by restoring a person's good reputation. Here is an appropriate prayer of St Benedict of Nursia (480-547)

> "O Lord, I place myself in your hands and dedicate myself to you. I pledge myself to do your will in all things: To love the Lord God with all my heart, all my soul, all my strength. Not to kill. Not to steal. Not to covet. Not to bear false witness. To honour all persons. Not to do to another what I would not wish done to myself. To chastise the body. Not to seek after pleasures. To love fasting. To relieve the poor. To clothe the naked. To visit the sick. To bury the dead. To help in trouble. To console the sorrowing. To hold myself aloof from worldly ways. To prefer nothing to the love of Christ. Not to give way to anger. Not to foster a desire for revenge. Not to entertain deceit in the heart. Not to make a false peace. Not to forsake charity. Not to swear, lest I swear falsely. To speak the truth

with heart and tongue. Not to return evil for evil. To do no injury: yea, even to bear patiently any injury done to me. To love my enemies. Not to curse those who curse me, but rather to bless them. To bear persecution for justice' sake. Not to be proud. Not to be given to intoxicating drink. Not to be an over-eater. Not to be lazy. Not to be slothful. Not to be a murmurer. Not to be a detractor. To put my trust in God. To refer the good I see in myself to God. To refer any evil in myself to myself. To fear the day of judgment. To be in dread of hell. To desire eternal life with spiritual longing. To keep death before my eyes daily. To keep constant watch over my actions. To remember that God sees me everywhere. To call upon Christ for defence against evil thoughts that arise in my heart. To guard my tongue against wicked speech. To avoid much speaking. To avoid idle talk. To read only what is good to read. To look at only what is good to see. To pray often. To ask forgiveness daily for my sins, and to seek ways to amend my life. To obey those in rightful authority in all things that are not sinful. Not to desire to be thought holy, but to seek holiness. To fulfil the commandments of God by good works. To love chastity. To hate no one. Not to be jealous or envious of anyone. Not to love strife. Not to love pride. To honour the aged. To pray for my enemies. To make peace after a quarrel, before the setting of the sun. Never to despair of your mercy, O God of Mercy. Amen."

CHAPTER SIXTEEN

SPIRITUAL GROWTH:
STEPS TEN TO TWELVE

STEP TEN

Step ten is about continuing the inventory during times of sobriety. In many ways it is the logical implication of steps six and seven when it says, "continued to take personal inventory and when we were wrong, promptly admitted it". This discipline counteracts the tendency of addicted people, who like Adam and Eve before them, tend to disown responsibility for their actions by blaming other people and circumstances as the real culprits. People in recovery learn to accept responsibility for their feelings and reactions. They acknowledge that while other people can trigger their emotional responses the causes lie within. For example, you didn't get a promotion recently. When your boss told you it was due to poor work performance, you disagreed, and because you were angry, you told him off. Working step ten doesn't mean that you don't get angry ever again. It means that you take responsibility for your anger, e.g. by acknowledging that your pride was hurt and that your reaction was an echo of how you felt when you failed to receive any affirmation from your father in childhood. When you become aware of these inward factors, you admit when you're wrong. So immediately after your outburst, you calm down and apologise to your boss for your inappropriate response. Step ten doesn't require you to go into a long explanation about why you're wrong or to make excuses. It requires only that you admit you're wrong.

We know that Bill Wilson was influenced by Ignatian spirituality, one aspect of which is known as the examen of consciousness, as distinct from an examination of conscience. Here is a shortened version which some people find helpful at day's end.

- Relax your body ...
- Calm your mind and imagination ...
- Affirm that God is present ...

Prayer for discernment
- "Father in heaven help me to recall with gratitude those occasions when I was aware of your presence today and to savour again what you meant to me (Pause for a moment's reflection).
- Help me to become aware of the promptings and inspirations you have given me today, and to know whether I responded to them or not (Pause for a moment's reflection).
- Enlighten my heart to recognise any unloving mood, attitude, desire, or action that saddened your Holy Spirit of love within me, today (Pause for a moment's reflection).

Conclude with the following prayer.

"Father in heaven, thank you for the gift of your Holy Spirit. Today it has urged me to see you more clearly, to love you more dearly and to follow you more nearly. As for my shortcomings, please forgive them and now, bless me as I sleep, so that refreshed, I may rise to praise you, through Jesus Christ our Lord. Amen."

STEP ELEVEN

As you know, 12 step programmes focus on the Higher Power. So it is not surprising to find that step 11 says, "Sought through prayer and meditation to improve our conscious contact with God as we understood Him, praying only for knowledge of His will for us and the power to carry that out." In his book *Will and Spirit: A Contemplative Psychology,* psychiatrist Gerald May says that transformation is a matter of moving away from the arbitrary control exercised by the wilful ego, to centres of power and value beyond itself. He described the two dispositions in these words: "Willingness implies a surrendering of one's self-separateness, an entering into, an immersion in the deepest processes of life itself. It is a realisation that one already is a part of some ultimate cosmic process and it is a commitment to participation in that process. In contrast, wilfulness is the setting of oneself apart from the fundamental essence of life in an attempt to master, direct, control, or otherwise manipulate existence."[80] So AA encourages recovering addicts to get a clearer sense of who God is and what God wants.

Over the years I have found that many people in recovery attend spirituality courses on topics such as, "Self-esteem and the love of God," "Healing the father and mother wound," and "Reducing Stress and Finding Peace". An addicted man or woman may have had a father who was physically or emotionally absent, or abusive. Or it may be that his or her mother was not able, for one reason or another to give him or her the love they needed. Not only do experiences of these kinds cause all kinds of emotional problems, they can inhibit the victim's ability to relate to God in a trusting way as a loving Father. As Mal. 4:6 says, "The hearts of fathers must be returned to the children and the hearts of the children to the fathers." Recovering addicts need to acknowledge those wounds, to forgive their fathers and mothers from the heart, whether they are living or dead, and if needs be to ask for prayer for healing of memories. This brings about inner healing, and opens the heart to God as a dear Father who says, "you are always with me, and everything I have is yours" (Lk 15:31). In his painting of the prodigal son's return, it is surely significant that artist Rembrant van Rijn depicted the Father's left hand as strong and masculine, while his right hand is soft and feminine. In other words, when a person in recovery is reconciled with his or her father and mother, they are also reconciled to the fatherly and motherly aspects of God's love.

Recovering addicts can also experience inner transformation as a result of scripture reading and prayer. In Eph 1:17, St Paul prays that God the Father, "may give you a spirit of wisdom and of revelation in the knowledge of him". In 2 Cor 3:18 he tells us how the prayer is

80   (San Francisco: Harper & Row, 1982), 6.

answered, "And we all, with unveiled face, beholding the glory of the Lord, are being transformed into the same image from one degree of glory to another. For this comes from the Lord who is the Spirit." We behold God's glory, first and foremost by contemplating the Person and purposes of God in the scriptures, e.g. by means of the four steps of *Lectio Divina,* namely by reading, reflecting, praying and contemplating God and God's word in the scriptures. Changed relationship with the Lord leads to a changed way of living. As Paul said in Col 3:9-10, "you have taken off your old self with its practices and have put on the new self, which is being renewed in knowledge in the image of its Creator."

Step 11 also encourages the person in recovery to seek out God's will. As Gal 5:18 says, "Be guided by the Spirit." With this in mind, St Paul wrote, "we have not ceased to pray for you, asking that you may be filled with the knowledge of his will in all spiritual wisdom and understanding" (Col 1:9). As a result many people in recovery can pray each morning:

"Father in heaven, yours is a Spirit of truth and love. Pour that same Holy Spirit into my body, my mind and my soul. Preserve me today from all illusions and false inspirations. Reveal your presence, your word and your will to me in a way I can understand, and I thank you that you will do this while giving me the ability to respond, through Jesus Christ our Lord. Amen."

I have written a book entitled, *Guided by God: Ordinary and Charismatic Ways of Discovering God's Will,* which you might find helpful in this regard.[81]

It can be noted in passing that it is sometimes possible that recovering addicts may also be oppressed by an evil spirit, in one way or another. Needless to say, discernment of spirits is necessary to establish whether deliverance prayer is needed. In his excellent book *Unbound,* Neal Lozano suggests that if an addicted person has good reason to think that a spirit or spirits are involved in the addiction, he or

---

81   (Luton: New Life, 2015).

she should not only renounce them, he or she should also command them to leave in the name of Jesus Christ. The following section of this book deal with that topic.

STEP TWELVE

One point that Bill Wilson and Dr Bob Smith discovered is the fact that an addict holds on to his or her sobriety by helping other addicts to attain and maintain sobriety. There is an Irish folk tale, which describes how, in the Autumn, a farmer stored seed potatoes in a large bin with a view to using them for the Spring sowing. He warned his wife not to use any of them. But when hungry people came to the door during the cold winter months, she felt sorry for them and gave each one a few potatoes from the bin. In the spring, when the time for sowing arrived, the woman was on tenterhooks because she knew that the bin was nearly empty. But when her husband opened it, surprise, surprise, it was full to the brim with first class seed potatoes! The message is obvious. In giving we receive, even to the point of miracles. As Jesus said in Lk 6:38, "Give, and it will be given to you. A good measure, pressed down, shaken together and running over, will be poured into your lap. For with the measure you use, it will be measured to you." To maintain and deepen one's sobriety, help others either to become or to remain sober.

CONCLUSION

A final point. Dr Gerald May warned that while some addicts break free of the addiction that enslaved them, they are in danger of becoming addicted to the Twelve Step programme, which is intended to be a means to transcendent freedom and not an end in itself. In his book *The Dark Night of the Soul*, he says wisely, "Later one may come to realise that recovery, as the most important thing in life, has become an idol. God was a means to an end – recovery. Then in the darkness, after the heart said yes and love grew, the idol of recovery teetered and fell. The powers had shifted. Recovery is now no longer the end, but only a means in the service of love."[82]

---

82   (San Francisco: Harper & Row, 2003), 163.

CHAPTER SEVENTEEN

RELATIVES, FRIENDS & COLLEAGUES OF ADDICTED PEOPLE

Two main points can be made about those who have a close relationship with addicted people. Firstly, they can and should try to help the addicted person to face reality and to seek the help he or she needs to recover. Secondly, often those who are close to an addicted person, e.g. children of an alcoholic, are badly affected by the experience and may have to seek the help they need to recover. As this is a big subject, and space is short, I will confine myself to a few comments.

A] *Crisis intervention*

Because they love the addicted person, family members, friends and colleagues can become what are known as enablers, people, who despite their desire to help, unwittingly facilitate the addicted person's dysfunctional behaviour. Here is a list of several clear signs that someone is enabling an addict's dysfunctional behaviour.

- Ignoring the addict's negative or potentially dangerous behaviour. This behaviour can involve anything from driving under the influence of drink or drugs, to failing to carry out familial and work responsibilities, while denying that a problem exists.
- Difficulty expressing emotions. Enablers are often unsure how to express their feelings such as fear or anger, especially if there are negative consequences for doing so, such as irrational and violent verbal or physical reactions.
- Prioritising the addict's needs before one's own. While it is natural to want to help loved ones, enabling takes helping a step too far, where the addict has his or her dysfunctional needs taken care of while the enabler neglects his or her own

legitimate needs. The scriptures say, "Love your neighbour as yourself" (Mk 11:31).

- Acting out of fear – Since addiction can cause frightening events, the enabler will do whatever it takes to avoid such situations.

- Lying to others in order to excuse the addict's behaviour, e.g. being dishonest when asked by an employer why the drinker is not at work.

- Blaming people or situations rather than the addict, e.g. a wife blaming her mother-in-law's inadequacies for her husband's addiction.

- As a result of the addicted person's dysfunction and unreasonable behaviour the enabler is likely to feel angry and hurt. Nevertheless, he or she continues to enable the addict's dysfunctional behaviour.

If you notice these behaviours in yourself or a loved one, realise that they may enable his or her addiction rather than helping to end it, as you intend. To stop being an enabler consider the possibility of taking these steps.

1. Engage in tough love. Leave messes as they are. Leave the addict to clean up the trouble he or she has caused while being irresponsible.

2. Get back autonomy. When possible, you should not allow the addict to put you in situations which may endanger yourself or others.

3. Help the addicted person see that his or her behaviour will have predictable consequences. Use a system similar to the use of a yellow or red card in soccer. In other words, specify what behaviour is unacceptable while describing its inevitable consequences, e.g. "If you are arrested, I will do nothing to bail you out," "I will not give you any more money in order to pay your debts," or "I will put you out of the house and seek a legal barring order."

4. Follow through with your resolutions no matter how difficult and painful they are. Rather than being cruel, you are expressing tough love which is motivated by a desire to help the addicted person, so that like the prodigal son in the parable, he or she might come to his or her senses and seek help in overcoming their problem. Do not agree to change your response unless clear and verifiable undertakings are abided by, e.g. going through a detoxification process and drug rehabilitation or joining a Twelve Step programme.

B] *Help for the victims of addicts*

Contemporary writing about those who live with an addicted person indicate that they are likely to become co-dependent. This subject is a large and complex one which will not be examined here in any depth. Suffice it to say that co-dependent relationships are a specific type of dysfunctional helping relationship. Broadly speaking, one person's help supports (enables) the other's under-achievement, irresponsibility, immaturity, addiction, procrastination, or poor mental or physical health. Some common symptoms of co-dependency are:

- intense and unstable interpersonal relationships
- inability to tolerate being alone, accompanied by frantic efforts to avoid being alone
- chronic feelings of boredom and emptiness
- subordinating one's own needs to those of the person with whom one is involved
- overwhelming desire for acceptance and affection
- perfectionism
- over-controlling
- dishonesty and denial
- manipulation
- lack of trust
- low self-worth.

In my experience the dependants of addicts, such as spouses and children, who are badly affected by addiction and co-dependency, can be helped by a variety of groups. Fortunately, they can assist such people to cope and recover from the ill-effects of the addiction of someone they love. The following groups are to be found in many places throughout the world:

1. Al-Anon Family Groups have one purpose: to help families of alcoholics. They do this by practicing the Twelve Steps, by welcoming and giving comfort to families of alcoholics, and by giving understanding and encouragement to them.

2. Al-ateen, is for teenage relatives and friends of alcoholics. Al-ateen is part of Al-Anon.

3. Adult Children of Alcoholics is intended to provide a forum for individuals who desire to recover from the effects of growing up in an alcoholic or otherwise dysfunctional family.

Many people have found that the many books of Melody Beattie on the subject of co-dependency are very helpful for recognising the problem, its many causes, and ways in which it can be overcome.

CONCLUSION

In the Easter liturgy, the original sin of Adam and Eve is referred to, in a paradoxical way, as a "happy fault", because it occasioned the coming of our redeemer in the person of Jesus Christ. All failings, including addictions, can become springboards to blessing and growth. As the Lord said to St Paul and to us in 2 Cor 12:9, "My grace is sufficient for you, for my power is made perfect in weakness." Knowing this to be the case, we can understand why Paul could say in 1 Thess 5:18, "in everything give thanks; for this is the will of God in Christ Jesus for you." In other words, even in the midst of addiction, we can thank God in the knowledge that the addiction is embraced by God's benevolent providence in such a way that, "Where sin abounds, grace abounds much more" (Rm 5:20). That is why Paul could say, "in all things [including addiction] God works for the good of those who love him" (Rm 8:28).

CHAPTER EIGHTEEN

THE SPREAD AND GROWTH OF
ALCHOHOLICS ANONYMOUS

In 1943, AA spread to Australia when a group was formed in Sydney. Fr Tom Dunlea, an Irish priest who was connected with AA in Sydney, visited Ireland in 1946. While in Dublin, he was interviewed by the *Evening Mail*. He spoke at some length about the success of the Sydney group of AA. His description of how the fellowship operated was not strictly accurate but, he was the first person to introduce AA to the general public in Ireland. At about the same time Conor F., an Irish American, visited Ireland from Philadelphia. He had been sober for three years and was determined to form an AA group in Dublin before he returned to the U.S. He met a non-alcoholic lady called Eva Jennings who arranged for him to meet a Dr Moore from St Patrick's Hospital who, in turn, put him in touch with Richard, a chronic alcoholic. Their coming together in November 1946 was the first AA meeting held in Ireland.

The venue for AA's first meeting in Great Britain was pretty classy -London's Dorchester Hotel. The meeting was held in Room 202 of the hotel at 8pm on Monday, 31st March 1947. By January 1949 meetings in London were being held on Tuesdays and Thursdays at 11 Chandos Street and membership had passed the magic 100.

Several of the tenets of what would eventually become AA's Twelve Traditions were first expressed by Bill Wilson in the Foreword to the First Edition of the *Big Book of Alcoholics Anonymous* in 1939. They provide guidelines for relationships between the Twelve-Step groups, members, other groups and society at large.

One – Our common welfare should come first; personal recovery depends upon AA unity.

Two – For our group purpose there is but one ultimate authority

– a loving God as He may express Himself in our group conscience. Our leaders are but trusted servants, they do not govern.

Three – The only requirement for AA membership is a desire to stop drinking.

Four – Each group should be autonomous except in matters affecting other groups, or AA as a whole.

Five – Each group has but one primary purpose – to carry its message to the alcoholic who still suffers.

Six – An AA group ought never endorse, finance or lend the AA name to any related facility or outside enterprise, lest problems of money, property and prestige divert us from our primary purpose.

Seven – Every AA group ought to be fully self-supporting, declining outside contributions.

Eight – Alcoholics Anonymous should remain forever non-professional, but our service centres may employ special workers.

Nine – AA, as such, ought never be organised, but we may create service boards or committees directly responsible to those they serve.

Ten – Alcoholics Anonymous has no opinion on outside issues, hence the AA name ought never be drawn into public controversy.

Eleven – Our public relations policy is based upon attraction rather than promotion; we need always maintain personal anonymity at the level of press, radio and films.

Twelve – Anonymity is the spiritual foundation of all our Traditions, ever reminding us to place principles before personalities.[83]

Clarence Snyder was another of the founding members of AA.

He and Annette Nelson from Tampa, Florida started the first "Came to Believe" retreats in 1966. The inspiration for the retreat format began in Akron, Ohio, when just a few AA members needed to find a way in which to attend to the large numbers of men seeking help. Synder later said the retreats were designed to give a recovering alcoholic/addict "a life-changing experience". He explained, "We went through our 12 steps at these weekend retreats." The Came To Believe retreats are conducted regularly in the USA, Britain and Ireland. They apply the methods and principles which were used during the beginning years of Alcoholics Anonymous. Having helped to conduct a couple such retreats, I know from experience how impressive and effective they can be. I also know that some members of the Fellowship are worried because they find that a number of the members are either indifferent to or even antagonistic to the emphasis on God and spiritual experience. The Came to Believe retreats help to preserve the great grace which had empowered the foundation of AA.

PART THREE

FREEDOM FROM OPPRESSIVE EVIL SPIRITS

CHAPTER NINETEEN

INTRODUCTION

I was born in 1945 at the end of World War II. As I grew up, I heard about the Holocaust. Descriptions of the greatest crime in history disturbed me deeply during my teenage and college years. I was ordained a priest in 1971. At that time, I suspected that references to the Devil were a metaphorical way of speaking about the dark side of the unconscious mind and the systemic evils inherent in the unjust and oppressive structures of society. I tended to understand the evil of the Holocaust in those reductionist and rationalistic terms. I even wrote an article for a clerical magazine in which I explained away the notion of possession in a psychological way.[84]

In 1972, I went to Germany on holidays with a priest friend of mine. We mainly got around by hitching lifts. On one occasion we were dropped off outside Dachau concentration camp, which is on the outskirts of Munich. Having visited the museum, we went to see the gas chambers and crematoria. Not only did they resurrect my troubled, adolescent feelings about the Holocaust, I seemed to have a direct, gut level sense of the mystery of evil as I stood there. At that moment I spontaneously felt that the Holocaust was demonic in origin, and that my sense of God was inadequate in comparison to such a horror. Providentially, a few days later my friend and I visited the Olympic Stadium where we met some Jesus People from the USA who were singing religious songs. While my friend spoke with some of them, I looked at religious books they were selling. Eventually, I bought, *The Cross and the Switchblade* by David Wilkerson.[85] It told the remarkable story of a Southern, Protestant clergyman who was led by the Spirit to work, sometimes in miraculous ways, with drug

---

84 "Possessed by a personal Devil?" in *The Furrow* (June 1974):334-5.
85 (London: Lakeland, 1976).

addicts in New York City. As I read it, I felt that David's God was the one I was looking for. One who was greater than the terrible evil that I had encountered in Dachau.

Some time later in 1974 I had a Pentecostal type experience when the God I had desired for two years became the God I experienced through an unmerited outpouring of the Holy Spirit. There was a great paradox implicit in that anointing. The more I became consciously aware of the incomprehensible love of God, the more I became aware of the insidious existence and activity of the Devil. I came to see that Cardinal Lustiger, a Jew by birth, and former Archbishop of Paris was correct when he said, "At the heart of the opponent's [Nazi] ideology was the persecution of the chosen people, the Jewish people, because they were a messianic people. When as a child I spent time in Nazi Germany, I had understood: Nazism's aim was more than Promethean; it was Satanic."[86] Hebrew Catholic, Roy H. Schoeman made a similar point in a section entitled, "Diabolical Motivations Behind the Holocaust," in *Salvation is From the Jews*.[87]

Ever since the mid-1970s I have been travelling in order to preach and to minister to people in Ireland and in many other countries. While I have witnessed wonderful things over the years, I have also observed a decline of belief in the supernatural, which has coincided with a growing apostasy. As greater numbers of people have drifted away from the Church, they live as if God does not exist. Paradoxically as this has happened, there has been increasing evidence of the malicious activity of the evil one all over Europe. Prof. Valter Cascioli, a psychologist and scientific consultant to the International Association of Exorcists, who lectures on the exorcist course in Regina Apostolorum Institute in Rome, acknowledged this when he said, "There is a broad spread of superstitious practices, and with that a growing number of requests for help from people who are directly or indirectly oppressed by evil."[88]

....

86   Jean-Louis Missika and Dominique Wolton, *Choosing God-Chosen by God* (San Francisco: Ignatius Press, 1991), 108.

87   (San Francisco: Ignatius, 2003), 245-249.

88   *The DailyTelegraph* (26 September 2016).

As a result of developments like these, I decided, beginning in the 1980s, to start writing about diabolical evil, notably in a book entitled, *Unveiling the Heart: How to Overcome Evil in the Christian Life*.[89] It had a pastoral and an apologetic aim. At a pastoral level it sought to deal with an important but neglected aspect of Christian spirituality. At an apologetic level, I knew that many non-church going people were morbidly fascinated by the phenomenon of evil. I hoped that a Christian treatment of the subject would introduce open-minded readers to the supernatural realm in a credible and quasi-empirical way. As a result of my writings and lectures in Trinity College, Maynooth University and Galway University, together with radio and TV interviews about evil spirits and exorcism, numerous people contacted me to ask for deliverance prayer. Unfortunately, I was unable to help many of them because of the sheer numbers involved. That grieved me then and now, because I have a strong conviction that deliverance ministry is an integral, if subordinate, aspect of the new evangelisation called for by the Church. As Jesus testified, "He has sent me to proclaim freedom for the prisoners... to set the oppressed free... if it is by the finger of God that I cast out demons, then the kingdom of God has come upon you" (Lk 4:18; 11:20). At the end of Mark's Gospel Jesus said to the apostles, and through them to us, "Go into all the world and proclaim the gospel to the whole creation... And these signs will accompany those who believe: in my name they will cast out demons" (Mk 16:15-17). Surely, it is significant, that the very first sign of the coming of the kingdom which Jesus mentioned was that of exorcising people.

It is my hope that this theological reflection will prove to be a modest response to words which were spoken by St Paul VI in 1972 when he said, "This matter of the Devil and of the influence he can exert on individuals as well as on communities, entire societies or events, is a very important chapter of Catholic doctrine which should be studied again, although it is given little attention today."[90]

---

89 (Dublin: Veritas, 1995).
90 "Deliver us from Evil," General audience of Pope Paul VI, Nov 15th 1972 as reprinted in *L'Osservatore Romano* (Nov 23rd 1972).

Although the Holy Father, penned those words so many years ago, there has been very little reaction in Ireland.

In February 2005 I had an article published in *The Furrow* which was entitled, "Things that go Bump in the Night."[91] It was about paranormal experiences and the Church's need to work out how to respond to them. The article evoked a huge response in the media, which indicated that the general public was fascinated by the subject. In January 2018, I felt led to write a letter to the bishops of Ireland. It too was published in *The Furrow*. Part of it was about the need to appoint trained exorcists in each diocese. Among other things I said, "To the best of my knowledge there are very few, if any, trained, officially appointed exorcists in Ireland. It breaks my heart to acknowledge this, because it means that there are so many afflicted people who, having had recourse to the Church for help, end up feeling let down and abandoned. When the majority of priests are consulted by a person who claims to be spiritually oppressed or possessed, they tend to feel ill-equipped to help them. If they encourage the afflicted people to contact the bishop's office for help, they often get little or no professional assistance. As a result, they are frequently referred on to the few people in the country who have a reputation, rightly or wrongly, for being able to deal with such cases. The truth is, every diocese has an evangelical and pastoral duty to have exorcism teams in order to help those who are oppressed or possessed by evil spirits. It is significant that when Jesus commissioned the apostles to go and preach the gospel, he said to them, 'these signs will accompany those who believe: In my name they will drive out demons' (Mk 16:17). It would seem therefore, that deliverance from evil spirits was one of the principal signs of the coming of the kingdom. You, our bishops, have made great progress in the area of safeguarding children and vulnerable adults. But surely the time has come to make an equally conscientious effort to deliver and protect people from the malicious and destructive activity of the enemy of their souls."[92]

---

91   Vol. 56, No. 2 (Feb., 2005): 94-98.

92   *The Furrow*, Vol. 69, No. 1 (Jan 2018): 29-30.

As a result of the letter's appearance, *The Irish Catholic* published an article entitled, "Combat Surge in Evil". It mentioned the need for trained exorcists.[93] It too evoked a huge response. As a result, many articles were written at home and abroad which reported what I had said. I also received innumerable requests to do interviews for newspapers, and magazines as well as many invitations to participate in radio and TV programmes in Ireland and as far away as the United States, and Romania. While I turned down the majority of those requests, I decided to write this book.

Up to half of *Freedom from Evil Spirits* focuses on how to be delivered from the malevolent influence of the devil. As a pastoral guide it is relatively brief. It does not pretend to be comprehensive or exhaustive. Although I know a certain amount about deliverance, I am painfully aware of how much I don't know, not only in a theoretical way, but more importantly at a practical, experiential level. I am also aware how true it is that people don't care how much you know until they know how much you care. Because I do really care, I felt that I should share what I already know in the hope that it might prove to be helpful to those who know even less than I do. Those who are interested in a more thorough treatment of the subject could look at one or more of the recommended books in the bibliography. As a Chinese proverb so rightly says, "a journey of a thousand miles begins with a single step."[94]

---

93   *The Irish Catholic*, (Jan 18th 2018), 1.
94   Philosopher Laozi (c. 604 BC - 531 BC) in the Tao Te Ching, chapter 64.

CHAPTER TWENTY

THE DEVIL & EVIL SPIRITS EXIST

Whereas up to 50% of Irish people believe in the devil's existence, only about 25% of our fellow Europeans do. The majority understand references to the evil one in rationalistic and reductionist terms which explain away the Devil and the world of evil spirits as a mere symbolic label for everything that threatens people in their subjectivity.

A few years ago, I travelled to the Ulster Television studios in Belfast to participate in a discussion on the existence or non-existence of the devil. For the sake of balance, the producers tried, in typical fashion, to ensure that the participants represented three different world views. Briefly put, world-views are conscious and unconscious assumptions that govern our interpretation of reality.

- The programme included a psychiatrist, a former Catholic, who argued in naturalistic terms that there was neither God, devil, or supernatural realm. For instance, she explained the devil away, in psychological terms, as nothing but a projection of the dark side of the human mind.

- There was a liberal Christian academic who accepted the existence of God, but explained the devil away as a mere myth that shouldn't be understood in literal, objective terms. The devil is another word for the evil effects of systemic injustice in the structures of society.

- For my part, I tried to affirm the existence of a supernatural realm, including the devil and evil spirits, and therefore the possibility of temptation, spiritual oppression and even, in rare cases, possession.

I believe that this third position is the one which is found in the New Testament, and the teaching of the Church.

SCRIPTURAL EVIDENCE

It is clear from the New Testament that Jesus was tempted by the devil and that he was an exorcist who freed people from demonic influences. He referred to the devil as "the ruler of this world" (Jn 16:30) and the "prince of this world" (Jn 14:30). Not only did Jesus teach his disciples to pray, "deliver us from the Evil One" (Mt 6:13) "he called his 12 disciples together and began sending them out two by two, giving them authority to cast out evil spirits" (Mk 6:7). On one occasion when "The 72 returned with joy, saying, 'Lord, even the demons are subject to us in your name,' he responded, 'I saw Satan fall like lightning from heaven. Behold, I have given you authority to tread on serpents and scorpions, and over all the power of the enemy, and nothing shall hurt you. Nevertheless, do not rejoice in this, that the spirits are subject to you, but rejoice that your names are written in heaven'." Years later in the post-resurrection era, St Peter testified: "God anointed Jesus of Nazareth with the Holy Spirit and with power; he went about doing good and healing all that were oppressed by the devil, for God was with him" (Acts 10:38). When Paul was converted, Jesus said to him, "I am sending you to open their eyes and turn them from darkness to light, and from the power of Satan to God" (Acts 26:17-18). In 2 Cor 4:4, St Paul acknowledged that Satan "is the *god of this world*" who has blinded the eyes of unbelievers.

VIEWS OF TWO EMINENT SCHOLARS

The late Raymond Brown was one of the greatest Catholic biblical scholars writing in English in the post Vatican II era. He clearly stated in a number of his books, such as *Responses to 101 Questions on the Bible,* in numbers 50 and 51, that he believed that the devil exists and that Jesus was an exorcist.[95] He said, "I would argue that it is almost impossible to understand Jesus' proclamation in word and deed of the coming of the kingdom of God without understanding at the same time the opposition that stems from a kingdom of evil already established in this world." Karl Rahner, possibly the greatest Catholic

---

95   (New York: Paulist Press, 1990), 70-71.

theologian of the 20th Century, taught that, rather than being merely assumed as some writers maintain, the devil's existence is dogmatically asserted by the Church. He wrote in *Sacramentum Mundi*, "It should be firmly maintained that the existence of angels and demons is affirmed in scripture and not merely assumed as a hypothesis which can be dropped today."[96] While Catholic theology believes that the devil and evil spirits do exist, it would not be committed to the mythological elements of the New Testament world view.

CHURCH TEACHING

Does the Church still teach that the devil exists? Yes and no. Cardinal Suenens said in his *Renewal and the Powers of Darkness*, "It is true that in the course of the centuries the existence of Satan and of the devils has never in fact been the object of an explicit declaration of her Magisterium."[97] But on the other hand, it is true to say that the Magisterium of the Church has often referred to the Devil. For example, a definition of the 4th Lateran Council categorically declared that evil has not existed from the beginning but that everything evil has temporal limits and arises from the free choices of creatures (Denzinger 428). It stated that God created Satan and the other devils as good angelic spirits but that they became evil by their own choice. Thus, this definition presupposes the existence of the devil. Pope Paul VI said during a General Audience on November 15th 1972, "It is a departure from the picture provided by biblical and Church teaching to refer to the devil's existence...as a pseudo reality, a conceptual and fanciful personification of the unknown causes of our misfortunes."[98] A document entitled, *Christian Faith and Demonology,* which was published by the Sacred Congregation for Divine Worship in 1975 stated, "We repeat, ... that though still emphasising in our day the real existence of the demonic, the

---

96   (London: Darton, Longman & Todd, 1983), 5.

97   "Devil" in *Sacramentum Mundi: An Encyclopedia of Theology,* vol. 2 (London: Burns & Oates, 1970), 73.

98   "Deliver us from Evil," General audience of Pope Paul VI, Nov 15th 1972 as reprinted in *L'Osservatore Romano* (Nov 23rd 1972).

Church has no intention...of proposing an alternative explanation which would be more acceptable to reason. Its desire is simply to remain faithful to the Gospel and its requirements."[99]

Speaking about exorcism par. 1673 of the *Catechism of the Catholic Church* said, "When the Church asks publicly and authoritatively in the name of Jesus Christ that a person or object be protected against the power of the Evil One and withdrawn from his dominion, it is called exorcism. Jesus performed exorcisms and from him the Church has received the power and office of exorcising. In a simple form, exorcism is performed at the celebration of Baptism... Illness, especially psychological illness, is a very different matter; treating this is the concern of medical science. Therefore, before an exorcism is performed, it is important to ascertain that one is dealing with the presence of the Evil One, and not an illness."

At the launch of the revised Rite of Exorcism in late 1999, Cardinal Estevez, of the Congregation of Divine Worship, reiterated the Church's teaching, "the existence of the devil is not an opinion...it belongs to Catholic faith and doctrine... but the strategy of the devil is to convince people that he does not exist." The cardinal then went on to suggest that the Devil's malign activity helps to explain particular atrocities, such as World War II and the Holocaust. He also stated in a more general way that the devil, "manages to trap many people - he fools them by leading them to believe that happiness can be found in money, power and sexual lust. He deceives men and women by persuading them that they do not need God and that they are self-sufficient."

POPE FRANCIS ON THE DEVIL

In a homily, which he delivered on the 4th October 2014, Pope Francis said, "Maybe some of you might say: 'But Father, how old fashioned you are to speak about the devil in the 21st Century!' But look out

---

99 "Christian Faith and Demonology" in *Vatican Collection II: More Post Conciliar Documents*, ed. Austin Flannery (Dublin: Dominican Publications, 1982), 476.

because the devil is present! The devil is here... even in the 21st Century! And we mustn't be naïve, right? *We must learn from the Gospel how to fight against Satan* [my italics]." He echoed that point when he wrote, "We should not think of the devil as a myth, a representation, a symbol, a figure of speech or an idea."[100] Speaking to priest participants on a Course on the Internal Forum organised by the Apostolic Penitentiary in 2017, Pope Francis made this observation, "When the confessor becomes aware of the presence of genuine spiritual disturbances... he must not hesitate to refer the issue to those who, in the diocese, are charged with this delicate and necessary ministry, namely, exorcists. But these must be chosen with great care and great prudence." In his Apostolic Exhortation, *The Call of Holiness in Today's World*, par. 160, Pope Francis wrote, "Satan is present in the very first pages of the Scriptures, which end with God's victory over the devil. Indeed, in leaving us the Our Father, Jesus wanted us to conclude by asking the Father to "deliver us from evil". That final word does not refer to evil in the abstract; a more exact translation would be "the evil one". It indicates a personal being who assails us. Jesus taught us to ask daily for deliverance from him, lest his power prevail over us." Therefore, it is not surprising to find that in 2014 Pope Francis gave formal recognition to the International Association of Exorcists, a group of 250 priests spread across 30 countries, who exercise the ministry of exorcism.

CONCLUSION: FROM ALIENTATION TO TRUE PERSONHOOD

Bishop Karol Wojtkyla attended the whole of Vatican ll (1962-1965). Not only did he describe it as the "seminary of the Holy Spirit," he made significant contributions to two of its most influential documents, *Dignitatis Humanae* and *Gaudium et Spes*. His best-known biographer, George Weigel, has pointed out in *Witness to Hope*, that the future Pontiff believed that the Christological anthropology implicit in pars 22 and 24 of *Gaudium et Spes*, was the theological linchpin of

---

100 Par. 162 of the Apostolic Exhortation, *Rejoice and be Glad.*

Vatican ll.[101] Professor Michael Waldstein, an expert on John Paul's theology of the body, shares Weigel's opinion.[102]

Pars 22 and 24 of *Gaudium et Spes* maintain that we can only know our deepest selves in and through self-giving relationships with Christ and one another. There is a good example of what John Paul had in mind in a *Conference on Prayer* by Thomas Merton. "Who am I?" he asked, "My deepest realisation of who I am is – I am one loved by God."[103] As a result of their rebellion against God, the fallen angels have no relationship with the divine and consequently suffer from a state of profound inner alienation not only from God but also from their true selves. The word diabolical is significant from an etymological point of view because it is derived from the Greek word *dia-bolos*, which literally means "to tear apart" (*dia-bollein*). Not surprisingly, therefore, there is something profoundly impersonal and schizophrenic about Satan and the personalities of those he oppresses. They are subject to inner disturbance, conflict and psycho-spiritual confusion. The Gerasene demoniac in Mk 5:1-17 & Lk 8:26-37, who was stripped of human dignity, acted violently and was out of control, epitomised the depersonalising and irrational activity of the evil one. Deliverance ministry, on the other hand, seeks to reconcile the person to his or her deepest spiritual self in and through reconciliation with God through Jesus Christ. To do this, many obstacles such as resentments, negative inner messages and distorted thinking have to be challenged, renounced and cast out.

---

101 (London: HarperCollins, 2005), 224.

102 *Man and Woman, He Created Them: A Theology of the Body* (Boston: Pauline Books & Media, 2006), 23.

103 Quoted by John J. Higgins, S.J., in *Thomas Merton on Prayer* (New York: Doubleday 1971), 62.

CHAPTER TWENTY-ONE

OVERCOMING TEMPTATION

The temptation to sin is a characteristic of every human life. In Genesis we are told how Adam and Eve were tempted by the devil in the Garden of Eden. Even Jesus, the Son of God, experienced such temptation in the wilderness (cf. Lk 4:1–13; Mt 4:1–11). Speaking about the three temptations of Jesus in the course of a general audience on the 22nd February 2012, Pope Benedict XVI said that Satan sought to draw Jesus from being a messiah of self-sacrifice to a messiah of power. During his period in the wilderness Jesus was exposed to danger and was assaulted by temptations which were far from God's plan because they involved power, success and domination rather than the total gift of self on the Cross. Heb 4:15, summed up the situation when it said, "For we do not have a high priest who is unable to empathise with our weaknesses, but we have one who has been tempted in every way, just as we are - yet he did not sin."

The English words tempt and temptation are derived from Latin and mean "to test" or "to try the strength of something". Theology says that while God may test a person's fidelity by allowing him or her to endure all kinds of trials, tribulations and temptations, God never does the tempting. As Scripture says, "No one when tempted should say, 'I am being tempted by God', for God cannot be tempted by evil, and God tempts no one" (Jm 1:13).

Temptation can have two main sources:

- Firstly, there are our own sinful desires. St James says, "each person is tempted when he is lured and enticed by his own desire" (Jm 1:14). In *De Diabolo Tentaton*, Homil. II, 1, St John Chrysostom wrote, "It is not the devil but people's own carelessness which causes all their falls and all the ills about which they complain."

- Secondly, the devil can tempt us. In Rev 12:17 we read that the evil one, "went off to make war on the rest of her (Mary's) offspring, on those who keep the commandments of God and hold to the testimony of Jesus." In his *Summa Theologiae*, St Thomas Aquinas says that the proper role of the devil is to tempt.[104]

HOW TO RESIST TEMPTATION

St Paul said in a reassuring way, "No temptation has overtaken you except what is common to mankind. And God is faithful; he will not let you be tempted beyond what you can bear. But when you are tempted, he will also provide a way out so that you can endure it" (1 Cor 10:13). I think we would have to say that this promise presupposes that the person being tempted is mature, self-aware, and utterly reliant on God. Because that isn't always the case, many people, despite their good intentions, do give in to temptation. The evil they wish to avoid is the very thing they do (cf. Rm 7:19).

There is an interesting example of this paradox in the gospels. St Peter loved Jesus. He promised to go to Jerusalem with him, and if necessary, to die with him. But Jesus knew his friend through and through. He responded, "Simon, Simon, listen! Satan has sought permission to sift all of you like wheat, but I have prayed for you that your faith may not fail; and you, when once you have turned back, strengthen your brothers" (Lk 22:31-33). Jesus knew that despite Peter's good intentions, Satan would exploit his weaknesses during passion week. Surprisingly, he didn't pray that Peter would overcome temptation. He knew that a fall was inevitable because the spiritual life of Peter was built on the sand of presumption and a lack of humble self-awareness. So he prayed instead, that when Peter had fallen, he would not be filled with such despairing self-contempt that like Judas, he would be so disillusioned that he would doubt the mercy and love of Jesus. In fact, Peter's fall not only taught him a lot about

---

104 In part 3, Question 41 of *The Summa Theologica*, Aquinas answers four questions about Christ's temptation.

himself and his weakness but also about the power and tactics of the evil one, who, as he testified, "prowls around like a roaring lion looking for someone to devour" (1 Pt 5:8). But he also learned that his betrayal of Jesus turned out to be a "happy fault" insofar as it evoked in him a heartfelt desire for the promised Holy Spirit, which filled him and the other apostles on Pentecost Sunday when God's power was made perfect in their weakness (cf. 2 Cor 12:9). No wonder Paul said in Rm 5:20, "where sin increased, grace increased all the more."

In 2 Cor 11:14, St Paul warned us that, "Satan himself masquerades as an angel of light." What he meant by this is that in the case of good people, the devil doesn't try to get them to commit serious sin because he knows his temptations would be in vain. What he does instead is that he tempts them with what is good in order to seduce them away from what is better. When St Ignatius of Loyola was studying in Barcelona, he found that his attention was being distracted by all kinds of spiritual insights. Eventually, he realised that the devil was using them in order to deflect him form his providential calling. As a result, St Ignatius wrote, "It is characteristic of the evil angel, who takes on the appearance of an angel of light, to enter by going along the same way as the devout soul and then to exit by his own way with success for himself. That is, he brings good and holy thoughts attractive to such an upright soul and then strives little by little to get his own way, by enticing the soul over to his own hidden deceits and evil intentions."[105] In our times the devil often gets people to focus in a compassionate way on the satisfaction of pressing needs in order to distract them from urgent priorities such as prayer, spending time with one's family or engaging in evangelisation. So discernment is needed, because all that glitters is not necessarily gold.

St Ignatius also believed that the devil tries to separate people from the Lord by tempting them to have an inordinate and idolatrous "love for money, a root of all kinds of evil (1 Tim 6:10). Then, the person becomes preoccupied with a desire for a good reputation,

---

105 *Spiritual Exercises* week two.

status, honours and influence. That leads to a desire for ethical independence. It is at this stage that relativistic and subjective views of right and wrong begin to predominate as the person engages in activities that are seriously sinful in God's eyes (cf. Ps 51:4) if not their own. In his *Spiritual Exercises*, St Ignatius said that in order to resist diabolical temptation, a believer needs to be familiar with the typical tactics of the Devil. He likes to operate as a bully who intimidates, a seducer who fosters secrecy, and as a military commander who exploits a person's principal vulnerability.

A] THE BULLY WHO INTIMIDATES

The devil comes on strong during temptation. He tries to intimidate us in order to produce a resigned defeatism in the heart. The weaker the person appears to be, the more the devil will try to bully him or her by piling on the pressure. But if, from the onset of the temptation, the person is firm and courageous in resisting his temptations, the devil is exposed as a coward. St Ignatius wrote, "it is the custom of the enemy to become weak, lose courage and turn to flight with his seductions as soon as one leading his or her spiritual life faces temptations boldly, and does exactly the opposite of what the enemy suggests. However, if one begins to be afraid and to lose courage in temptations, no wild animal on earth can be more fierce than the enemy of our human nature."[106] This advice is particularly relevant during times of desolation, when the inner sense of God's presence can be eclipsed and we are troubled by feelings like restlessness, aridity, sadness and hopelessness. It is just when we arrive at our lowest ebb that the enemy will attack. It is then, too, that we need to recall that "the spirit you received is not a spirit of cowardice but rather the spirit of power and self-control" so "resist the devil and he will flee from you" (2 Tim 1:7; Jm 4:7). The great spiritual writers counsel that it is important to resist temptation as soon as it begins. Thomas à Kempis wrote in *The Imitation of Christ*, "We must be watchful, especially in the beginning of temptation, because it is then that the enemy is more easily

---

106   *The Spiritual Exercises*, Rule XII.

overcome if he is not allowed to come in through the door of the soul, but instead is kept out and resisted from the first knock... Withstand at the beginning, remedies afterwards come too late."[107]

B] *THE SEDUCER WHO LIKES SECRECY*

The evil one prefers to work in secret. Like a married man who has seduced a young woman, or *visa versa*, he will urge the person he tempts not to tell confessors, friends or confidants about his temptations. He will suggest that this is the best policy either because they wouldn't understand, or because they would be too harsh, too busy, or too lax. And he knows, says Ignatius, that "he cannot succeed in his evil undertaking once its obvious deceptions have been revealed... But if one reveals them to a good confessor or a spiritual person with knowledge of such deceits and malicious intentions, the evil one would be quite vexed, knowing that it cannot succeed in this evil undertaking once its obvious deceptions have been revealed."[108] And so in a time of temptation, it is a prudent thing to reveal one's struggle, no matter how shameful or embarrassing it might be, to a person who is experienced in the area of discernment of spirits. St Vincent De Paul once wrote, "if anyone feels troubled by ideas which seem to be in some way misleading, are upset by acute anxiety or temptation, he should tell a spiritually experienced person, such as a spiritual director, so that the matter can be competently dealt with."[109]

C] *THE MILITARY COMMANDER WHO EXPLOITS WEAKNESS*

The devil is like a good military commander. He exploits a person's greatest vulnerability, especially during times of desolation. The enemy of our human nature, says Ignatius, "explores from every side all our virtues of intellect, faith and morals. Where he finds our defence is weakest and most deficient in regard to eternal salvation, it is at

---

107 *The Imitation of Christ,* chapter XXIII.

108 *The Spiritual Exercises,* Rule XIII

109 St Vincent de Paul, Common Rules, chapter 2, par. 2, in *Constitutions and Statutes of the Congregation of the Mission,* (Philadelphia: General Curia of the Congregation of the Mission, 1989), 107-8.

that point that the enemy attacks, trying to overcome us."[110] Psychologists have suggested that each personality type has a characteristic weakness. For example, those with a sanguine temperament are inclined to sensuality; those with a melancholic temperament incline to sadness and depression; those with a choleric temperament incline to anger and insensitivity; and those with a phlegmatic temperament incline to apathy and laziness. Devotees of the controversial Enneagram maintain that there are nine personality types. Each one is said to have a characteristic blind spot or obsession, e.g. an inordinate desire to avoid anger, pain, a sense of need, failure, ordinariness, emptiness, non-conformity, vulnerability and conflict. Mature Christians need the kind of self-awareness that recognises where God's protection is most needed. Otherwise they will be caught unawares. Afterwards they may confess in dismay, "I didn't know what came over me, it wasn't like me to do something like that." As St Paul admitted, "For I do not do the good I want to do, but the evil I do not want to do - this I keep on doing" (Rm 7:19). Once we grow in self-knowledge, however, we will be aware from personal experience which occasion of sin we most need to prayerfully avoid. As Jesus said to the apostles in Gethsemane, "Keep watch and pray, so that you will not give in to temptation. For the spirit is willing, but the body is weak!" (Mt 26:41).

SELF-DENIAL AND TEMPTATION

Jesus said, "If anyone desires to come after Me, let him *deny himself*, and take up his cross, and follow Me" (Mt 16:24). We can curb and counteract the selfish, self-indulgent inclinations of our nature, by engaging in such things as voluntary fasting and almsgiving. We can also renounce satisfactions, sensual, imaginative and intellectual, which may not be sinful in themselves. In this way the spiritual self is strengthened. Then, when temptation comes, we are better able to resist it, with the help of the Holy Spirit. As Jesus said to the apostles when they asked him why they had been unable to overcome the influence of the evil one who was oppressing a boy, he said, "this kind

110 *The Spiritual Exercises*, Rule XIV

can only be overcome through prayer and fasting," i.e. by acts of self denial (Mk 9:29). At the end of a talk on confronting the power of the devil, in 1972, Pope Paul VI said, "The Christian must be a militant; he must be vigilant and strong; and he must at times make use of special ascetical practices to escape from certain diabolical attacks. Jesus teaches us this by pointing to 'prayer and fasting' as the remedy. And the Apostle suggests the main line we should follow: 'Be not overcome by evil, but overcome evil with good'."[111]

---

111 "Deliver us from Evil," General audience of Pope Paul VI, Nov 15th 1972 as reprinted in L'Osservatore Romano (23rd November, 1972).

CHAPTER TWENTY-TWO

PSYCHOLOGY & DELIVERANCE

Besides suffering from psychological and physical problems, some people suffer from spiritual oppression and even possession by evil spirits. When people are *oppressed,* they suffer from a kind of spiritual neurosis where only part of their personality is subject to demonic influence. For instance, the devil can fill their minds with irrational thoughts, evil inclinations, illusions and false inspirations such as a compulsive inclination to engage in immoral sexual or financial behaviour, or an impulse to commit suicide. When people are *possessed,* and I have to say it is a very rare occurrence, they suffer from a form of spiritual psychosis because the devil seems to take over their entire personalities.

Oppression can be overcome by means of:

- Self-deliverance (which can be engaged in by any oppressed person)
- Simple exorcism (which can be performed by lay people)

Possession can be overcome by means of:

- Solemn exorcism (which can only be performed by a priest appointed by the bishop)

We will look at each of these below. But before doing so a word about the relationship between psychology and spirituality.

PSYCHOLOGY AND DELIVERANCE

People who no longer believe in a supernatural dimension to life often will explain demonic activity in purely psychological terms. If they are followers of Carl Jung, they will argue that evil spirits are really symbolic ways of talking about the shadow and complexes. For Jung the shadow referred to everything which a person was not fully conscious of, namely the inferior, rejected, "dark side" of the personality which could be projected on to others. As a result, people would see and reject in them what they failed to see and accept in themselves. Complexes are unconscious feelings, thoughts and memories that cluster together to form an independent and powerful mini personality or personalities. Jung wondered whether complexes, "might not be a description of primitive demonology."[112] Toward the end of his life, he concluded that there was more to the demonic than the shadow or complexes. Writing to the founder of Alcoholics Anonymous he said, "I am strongly convinced that... an ordinary person unprotected by an action from above, and isolated in society, cannot resist the power of evil, which is very aptly called the devil."[113] On another occasion he said at the end of World War II, "just when people were congratulating themselves on having abolished evil spirits, it turned out that instead of haunting the attic or old ruins, the spirits were flitting about in the heads of apparently normal Europeans."[114]

Followers of Sigmund Freud argue that the demonic is nothing but a way of talking about the *id* or instinctual self. He believed that the neuroses of olden times were masquerading in demonical shape and that evil spirits were the projection of the repressed impulses of the largely unconscious, instinctual self. He wrote, "The states of possession correspond to our neuroses, for the explanation of which we once more have recourse to psychical powers... We merely eliminate the projection of these mental entities into the external world which the middle ages carried out; instead, we regard them as having arisen in the patient's internal life, where they have their abode."[115] On another occasion he said, "The devil is certainly nothing else than the

---

112 Carl Jung, *Collected Works*, 8, para., 712.

113 Letter of Bill Wilson to Carl Jung Jan 23rd 1961. It is mentioned in the *Big Book* (New York: Alcoholics World Services, 2001), 26-27.

114 *Collected Works of Carl Jung, Civilization in Transition*, vol., 10, in "After the Catastrophe" (New Jersey: Princeton University Press, 1970), 194.

115 Sigmund Freud, 'A Seventeenth-Century Demonological Neurosis', in *The Standard Edition of the Complete Psychological Works*, Vol. IX (London: Hogarth Press, 1954), 71.

personification of the repressed instinctual life."[116] This statement is at once dogmatic and reductionist. It makes an unjustifiable logical jump from subjective psychological experience to an emphatic philosophical conclusion about the objective state of spiritual reality. This is what is called a category error, i.e. one in which things belonging to a particular category are presented as if they belong to a different category, e.g. something ontological being explained in a psychological way.

So much for the psychology of Jung and Freud. It would probably be true to say that many troubled people mistakenly attribute their afflictions to the activity of evil spirits when in fact they are psychological in origin, e.g. multiple personality disorder (which is also known as Dissociative Identity Disorder) and conditions such as zoopathy (the belief that an animal is dwelling in one's abdomen), Tourette's syndrome, schizophrenia, hysteria, some forms of epilepsy, psychasthenia and psychotic, bi-polar and depressive disorders.[117] As Abbott McCorkell has written, "I find a good number of people too readily attributing to the evil spirit situations that could be the result of other factors, e.g. psychological disorders or even physical conditions... There are also a good number who are quick to jump on a sort of "bandwagon" that is branded diabolical."[118]

The truth is, there is a reciprocal relationship between psychiatry and spirituality. Brazilian author Norberto Keppe has written: "Both exorcists and psychiatrists, working in isolation, have erred in their

----

116 Sigmund Freud, *Leonardo Da Vinci and a Memory of his Childhood* (New York: W W Norton & Co, 1964), 123.

117 For more on this subject, see, Adam C. Blai, "Medical and Mental Illness" in *Possession, Exorcism, and Hauntings* (GB: Amazon, 2014), 41-44; Mike Driscoll, "Demonic Attack or Mental Disorder?" in *Demons, Deliverance and Discernment*, (El Cajon, Calif: Catholic Answers, 2015), 55-67; and Cardinal Joseph Suenens, "The Renewal and the Casting out of Demons: Psychological Observations," in *Renewal and the Powers of Darkness* (London: Darton, Longman & Todd, 1983), 83-87.

118 Quoted by William J. Sneck, S.J., "Evil and the Psychological Dynamics of the Human Person," in *Deliverance Prayer*, ed. Linn & Linn (New York: Paulist Press, 1981), 114.

evaluations of mental illness because they have failed to perceive the mix of physical and spiritual symptoms presented by their patients. In fact, any pathology contains both physical and spiritual components because human beings contain the two elements of body and spirit. This illustrates the need to apply this knowledge to pathological situations. Medical schools and theological seminaries urgently need to address these two aspects of human illness if they wish to better understand and treat humanity because we have suffered setbacks in both areas. What is separated fools us becauase it splits the whole and obliges the scientist to divide the indivisible."[119]

Not surprisingly, therefore, the introduction to the new *Rite of Exorcism* (1999) says that exorcism should only be tried "after diligent inquiry and after having consulted experts in spiritual matters and, if felt appropriate, experts in medical and psychiatric science who have a sense of spiritual reality." In par. 160 of his Apostolic Exhortation, *Rejoice and be Glad*, Pope Francis wrote, "the biblical authors had limited conceptual resources for expressing certain realities, and in Jesus' time epilepsy, for example, could easily be confused with demonic possession. Yet this should not lead us to an oversimplification that would conclude that all the cases related in the Gospel had to do with psychological disorders and hence that the devil does not exist or is not at work."

Fr Joseph de Tonquedec, S.J., a well known French exorcist in Paris, once said, "Address the devil, and you will see him, or rather, not him but a portrait made up of the sick person's ideas of him."[120] In other words the symptoms of people suffering from psychological problems may express themselves as a need for exorcism in cultures, such as ours, where this notion is prevalent as a result of traditional religious beliefs and movies about exorcism. This is what can be called pseudo-possession. I saw it vividly illustrated when I was ministering in Italy. A priest who had invited me to preach at a conference had a

119 *Psychotherapy and Exorcism* (Sao Paulo: Proton Editora, 2018), 114.
120 Quoted by Cardinal Joseph Suenens in *Renewal and the Powers of Darkness* (London: Darton, Longman & Todd, 1983), 84.

strong and sometimes misguided preoccupation with the activity of evil spirits. One incident illustrated the point. During the conference an apparently possessed woman was brought to the priest for prayer by her husband and relatives. She was wrapped in a blanket. When she was uncovered, she undoubtedly had a very strained and pale appearance. My host felt that she needed a simple exorcism, as did her family. He prayed over her for some time in a loud, booming voice, but his prayers seemed to have little or no effect. I strongly suspected that the poor woman wasn't possessed or oppressed but merely depressed. I asked to speak to her with the help of an interpreter. I told her, that God loved her. I asked her about her feelings and she confirmed that she was suffering from depression and anxiety. With her consent I prayed for inner healing, and all her psychosomatic agitation ceased and she became completely peaceful. She remained that way for the rest of the conference. So discernment is always needed. That incident reminded me of something that St Jane the Chantal recounted about her friend St Francis de Sales, "About ten years before his death, and for a period of about two years, possessed people were very often brought to him – or at least they thought they were possessed – and when they left him they were healed or greatly comforted. When I heard the talk about these possessed people, I asked the Blessed to tell me what was happening and with great humility and modesty, he said, 'These people are good souls, who are suffering from some kind of depression. I hear their confession, give them communion, comfort them as best I can and tell them they are cured; they believe what I say and go their way in peace.' I have heard that hundreds of people afflicted like this were cured."[121] Although St Francis explained all these cases in psychological terms, it is possible that a person with an identifiable psychological problem could also be oppressed by evil spirits.

Over the years I have found that many of the people who contact me to ask for deliverance prayer insist that their problems are due to the activity of evil spirits. When I suggest that their lack of

121 *St Francis de Sales: A Testimony by St. Jane de Chantal*...introduction by Elisabeth Stopp. (London: Faber, 1967), 150.

inner peace may be psychological in origin, while suggesting that they should be assessed by a qualified psychologist or psychiatrist, they take umbrage while insisting that they know for sure that they are oppressed by evil spirits. Although they have contacted me, presumably because they think I know something about the subject of spiritual oppression and possession, nevertheless many of them reject my advice when it doesn't fit in with their own preconceived and often uninformed ideas. Sometimes they believe that deliverance prayer will act like the wave of a magic wand which will banish their problems, thereby saving them from having to engage in the long and challenging process of inner transformation that would enable them to recover their mental health.

THE NEED FOR DISCERNMENT OF SPIRITS

There is no doubt that discernment of spirits is essential in the ministry of deliverance in order to distinguish problems which are psychological in origin from those that are spiritual. Pope Francis has a very interesting chapter in his Apostolic Exhortation, *Rejoice and be Glad*, entitled, "Spiritual Combat, Vigilance and Discernment". In par. 166, he wrote, "How can we know if something comes from the Holy Spirit or if it stems from the spirit of the world or the spirit of the devil? The only way is through discernment, which calls for something more than intelligence or common sense. It is a gift which we must implore. If we ask with confidence that the Holy Spirit grant us this gift, and then seek to develop it through prayer, reflection, reading and good counsel, then surely we will grow in this spiritual endowment." In par. 170, Pope Francis went on to add, "Certainly, spiritual discernment does not exclude existential, psychological, sociological or moral insights drawn from the human sciences. At the same time, it transcends them. Nor are the Church's sound norms sufficient. We should always remember that discernment is a grace."

I have written about the subject of discernment in two books in particular.[122] I may say that I have found that the following quote of St John Eudes (1601–1680) has helped me for some time now to distinguish the spirit of the world from the spirit of Jesus. In his *The Life and the Kingdom of Jesus in the Soul,* the French saint wrote: "The laws and maxims of Jesus are very mild and holy and reasonable. The standards of the world are laws and maxims of Hell, and are diabolical, tyrannical and finally unbearable. The life of Jesus is a holy life made beautiful by all kinds of virtues; the life of the world is a depraved life, full of disorder and of all sorts of vice. The Spirit of Jesus is a spirit of light, of truth, of piety, of love, confidence, zeal and reverence for God and for all that belongs to God; the spirit of the world is a spirit of error, of unbelief, of darkness, of suspicion, of dissatisfaction, of impiety, of irreverence and hardness of heart towards God and all the things of God. The spirit of Jesus is a spirit of humility, of modesty, of self-distrust, of mortification and abnegation, of constancy and of firmness. But the spirit of the world is, by contrast, a spirit of pride, presumption, disordered self-love, fickleness and inconstancy. The spirit of Jesus is a spirit of mercy, charity, patience, gentleness and of unity with others. But the spirit of the world is a spirit of vengeance, envy, impatience, anger, slander and disunion. Finally, the spirit of Jesus is the spirit of God, a holy and divine spirit, filled with every grace, virtue, and blessing. It is a spirit of peace and tranquillity, which seeks nothing but the interests of God and of His greater glory. The spirit of the world, on the contrary, is the spirit of Satan, for it necessarily follows that, since Satan is the prince of this world, the world is animated and governed by his spirit - an earthly, carnal and animal Spirit; a spirit motivating all kinds of sin and accursedness; a spirit of unrest and anxiety, of storms and tempests, a spirit seeking only its own convenience, satisfaction and interests."[123]

....

122 Pat Collins, C.M., "Discernment of Spirits," in *Unveiling the Heart: How to Overcome Evil in the Christian Life* (Dublin: Veritas, 1995), 96-105; *Guided by God: Ordinary and Charismatic Ways of Discovering God's Will* (Luton: New Life, 2015), 145-148.

123 (CreateSpace Independent Publishing Platform, 2013), part 1, sec. 6.

Conclusion

The website of the United States Conference of Catholic Bishops (US-CCB) includes an informative section entitled, "Frequently Asked Questions about Exorcism". Speaking about the intersection of psychology and deliverance it says, "As part of the evaluation process (which can be established in a diocesan protocol), the afflicted member of the faithful should avail himself/herself of a thorough medical and psychological/psychiatric evaluation. Frequently, individuals present themselves claiming to be afflicted in any number of ways. Historically, however, the Church has exercised caution when evaluating such individuals for fear of unnecessarily drawing attention to the machinations of the devil or giving credit where no credit is due."

CHAPTER TWENTY THREE

HOW THE DEVIL CAN GET A FOOTHOLD

In Eph 4:27 St Paul counseled, "do not give the devil a foothold." Unfortunately, however, in contemporary society many people are rendered vulnerable to the influence of the devil for a number of reasons. Here are some common ones.

Many people have lost faith in the existence and influence of the devil. They argue that the idea of the evil one is an outdated myth from a pre-scientific age. As Bishop Fulton Sheen said in 1958, "Very few people believe in the devil these days which suits the devil very well. He is always helping to circulate the news of his own death. The essence of God is existence, and He defines Himself as: 'I am Who am.' The essence of the devil is the lie, and he defines himself as: 'I am who am not.' Satan has very little trouble with those who do not believe in him; they are already on his side."[124] So the Devil has managed to pass himself off as an anachronism, which is his greatest act of cunning. Needless to say, such denial does not change objective reality and leaves people wide open to demonic activity.

Nowadays large numbers of people are practical atheists in so far as they live as if God does not exist. They are inclined to revere the golden calf of possessions, pleasure, popularity and power in an idolatrous way. They tend to rewrite the commandments to suit themselves and, as a result, engage in activities that are seriously sinful in God's eyes, if not their own. This is particularly obvious in the whole realm of finances and sexuality, where so many Christian people ignore the ethical teachings of the scriptures and the Church. Not surprisingly, that form of willfulness, which leads to repeated sin of an objectively grave nature, can give evil spirits who "prowl around like a roaring lion looking for someone to devour" (1 Pt 5:8-9), a foothold into the person's life.

....

124 Fulton Sheen, *Life of Christ* (New York: Image, 2008), 67.

The scriptures give the impression that sin is a real barrier to salvation. As St Peter stated, "It is difficult for good people to be saved; what, then, will become of godless sinners?" (1 Pt 4:18). In spite of that fact, many of our contemporaries are universalists. They believe that the road that leads to heaven is wide and that most people take it. They believe this in spite of the fact that Jesus said the opposite in Mt 7:13. This misguided attitude to sin is undoubtedly contributing to the vulnerability of Christians to the subtle tactics of the evil one.

There are other people who may have been severely traumatised in the past, e.g. by disturbing events such as physical, psychological, spiritual or sexual abuse. Not surprisingly experiences like these naturally evoke a protective type of anger. If victims do not deal in a forgiving way with the causes of their anger and other negative feelings they can turn to feelings of resentment, vindictiveness, vengefulness, and hate. Clearly, they are un-godly emotional attitudes because the Lord is unconditionally merciful and loving. That being so, negative antagonistic attitudes, albeit unconscious ones, can provide the devil with an entry point.

G. K. Chesterton is believed to have said, "When people stop believing in God, it is not that they believe in nothing, they believe in everything."[125] I have found in Britain and Ireland that as people drift away from orthodox Christian belief, they begin to become involved in all kinds of occult and New Age ideas together with superstitious practices such as astrology, palmistry, spiritualism, Reiki, kundalini, fortune telling, contacting the dead, consulting mediums, and using a Ouija board or tarot cards in a misguided effort to contact the world of spirits or to gain control over their lives and their futures. By engaging in these and similar activities, people can unwittingly open

---

125 Dr Pasquale Accardo of New York tracked the quote back to its earliest known appearance in the 1937 study of Chesterton by Emile Cammaerts, *The Laughing Prophet: The Seven Virtues & G. K. Chesterton* (London: Methuen, 1937). It took the following form: "The first effect of not believing in God is to believe in anything."

themselves to the influence of evil spirits. Pars 2116-2117 of the *Catechism of the Catholic Church* state:

> "All forms of *divination* are to be rejected: recourse to Satan or demons, conjuring up the dead or other practices falsely supposed to 'unveil' the future. Consulting horoscopes, astrology, palm reading, interpretation of omens and lots, the phenomena of clairvoyance, and recourse to mediums all conceal a desire for power over time, history, and, in the last analysis, other human beings, as well as a wish to conciliate hidden powers. They contradict the honour, respect, and loving fear that we owe to God alone. All practices of *magic* or *sorcery*, by which one attempts to tame occult powers, so as to place them at one's service and have a supernatural power over others - even if this were for the sake of restoring their health – are gravely contrary to the virtue of religion. These practices are even more to be condemned when accompanied by the intention of harming someone, or when they have recourse to the intervention of demons. Wearing charms is also reprehensible. *Spiritism* often implies divination or magical practices; the Church for her part warns the faithful against it. Recourse to so-called traditional cures does not justify either the invocation of evil powers or the exploitation of another's credulity."

The use of magic-spells and curses of all kinds is based on the belief that it is possible to enlist the support of superhuman beings (evil spirits) and to persuade them to carry out the supplicant's wishes. They may have been focused on a family member in a previous generation and inherited by a relative in the present, or they may be the result of the present day malice and ill-will of someone who bears a grudge.

Surprising as it may seem, some people actually make a Faustian deal with the devil in order to be empowered to do something or to gain some desired advantage. For example, I have heard how a man in another country gave his soul to the devil in order to have great physical strength and high intelligence. By all accounts his desire was fulfilled.

The devil, as Jesus warned, is a liar and the truth is not in him (cf. Jn 8:44). Speaking of some people St Paul said, "you were far away from God and were his enemies because of the evil things you... *thought*" (Col 1:21). People, whose minds are full of misguided thinking and attitudes can become mental strongholds, characterised by false beliefs and attitudes such as, "you are unlovable," "you can never be forgiven," "there is no hope for you," and the like. Not only does the devil foster such thinking, which may have its roots in a difficult childhood or adult traumas, he will use such thinking as a foothold to gain an entry into a person's life.

There can be ungodly soul ties in a person's life as a result of illicit sexual relationships and practices, which may have involved extra marital promises commitments and agreements. Pornography, which is so freely available nowadays, can also create soul ties to the images and people being viewed. Not surprisingly, the devil can exploit these soul ties, e.g. in the form of harmful addictions.

Increasing numbers of people, who have failed to form an intimate relationship with Jesus, may get interested and involved in false beliefs, e.g. pantheism and reincarnation, or practices, like yoga and transcendental meditation, as well as non-Christian spiritualities of an esoteric, Gnostic kind. By unwittingly breaking the first commandment, such a person may open his or her heart, not to God, but to fallen angels who can use non-Christian beliefs in order to insinuate themselves into people's lives.

I know that some readers who espouse modern relativist views believe that all religions are equally valid paths to spirituality and to God. As a result they will take exception to what I have said here, believing it is intolerant and even arrogant. But this is the attitude of the Bible which is inspired, e.g. Ps 96:5 warns, "For all the gods of the Gentiles are devils;" Deut 32:16-17 says that when the Jews sacrificed to pagan Gods, "They sacrificed to demons which were no gods;" and again in Bar 4:6-8, we read, "For you provoked him who made you, by sacrificing to demons and not to God." Tertullian (160-229) believed that because pagan gods were supposedly deified human beings, they weren't real. Instead, their names and images "were employed by unclean spirits, and fallen angels . . . in order to take honour upon themselves and from God."[126]

On the other hand, 1 Tim 2:5 says, "For there is one God and one mediator between God and mankind, the man Christ Jesus;" and in Acts 4:12, St Peter proclaimed, "There is salvation in no one else! God has given no other name under heaven by which we must be saved." Experience teaches that to get involved in such things as New Age Spirituality and non-Christian religions can open the door to the influence of evil spirits.

---

126 As T.D. Barnes notes in his study of Tertullian he drew his understanding directly from Roman scholar Marcus Terentius Varro who believed that the gods of the Greco-Roman empire were simply deified men.

CHAPTER TWENTY-FOUR

SELF-DELIVERANCE

A few years ago I read a book entitled, *The Holy Spirit: Unbounded Gift of Joy*, in which Mary Ann Fatula, O.P., said that if a person feels oppressed by an evil spirit, he or she can say a prayer of self-deliverance.[127] This point introduced me to the notion of self-exorcism. Before looking at it, firstly here are a few preliminary questions.

A) *QUESTIONS TO ASK YOURSELF:*

The Church teaches that most of the afflictions that people attribute to evil spirits are psychological in origin. Are you on medication, e.g. for depression, anxiety, bi-polar disorder, or schizophrenia? Are you absolutely sure that your problems are not coming from your unconscious? Have you been assessed by a professional psychologist or psychiatrist?

If you are convinced that you are dealing with some form of evil spirit, do you think you are oppressed or possessed? What are your reasons for thinking this?

I have mentioned nine ways in which evil spirits can gain a foothold in a person's life. Would any of them apply to you? Remember, it is important to diagnose the origin of the problem if you want to apply the appropriate remedy.

B) *SOME USEFUL THINGS TO DO*

When you have identified how and when the evil spirits got a foothold in your life ask yourself, were you partly responsible? If so repent by telling God you are sorry for any past wrongdoing in the firm belief that you will be forgiven unconditionally. If you have never invited Jesus into your life, do so now by saying this so-called Miracle Prayer slowly and with heartfelt conviction.

127   (Collegeville: Liturgical Press, 1998), 113.

"Lord Jesus, I come before you, just as I am. I am sorry for my sins, please forgive me for them all, in your name; I forgive all others for what they have done against me. I renounce Satan, and his evil spirits, and all their works. I give you my entire self, Lord Jesus, now and forever. I invite you into my life Jesus. I accept you as my personal Lord and Saviour. Heal me, and change me, strengthen me in my body, soul and spirit. Come Lord Jesus, cover me with your precious blood, and fill me with your Holy Spirit, I love you Lord Jesus. I praise your holy name. I shall follow you every day of my life. Amen."

If you can identify any wrong attitude, inclination, feeling or action, firstly repent by seeking God's forgiveness ideally in the sacrament of reconciliation and then rebuke it in the name of Jesus, e.g.

"I rebuke you spirit prompted suicidal thoughts, feelings of worthlessness, resentment, lust, or the occult in the name of the Lord Jesus Christ."

Then be your own exorcist by commanding the spirits to leave your life, e.g.

"I command you, spirit by prompted suicidal thoughts, or feelings of worthlessness, resentment, lust, or the occult to leave me in the name of the Lord Jesus Christ."

As St Paul assures us, "For though we live in the world, we do not wage war as the world does. The weapons we fight with are not the weapons of the world. On the contrary, they have divine power to demolish strongholds (i.e. those of Satan). We demolish arguments and every pretension that sets itself up against the knowledge of God, and we take captive every thought to make it obedient to Christ" (2 Cor 10:3-6). If you have any object connected with the occult or New Age, such as a crystal, amulet, charm, etc., get rid of it.

If you feel that you have been the victim of a present day or generational curse, bless the person/s who may have targeted you or your ancestors. As Rm 12:4 says, "Bless those who persecute you. Don't curse them; pray that God will bless them." You could say this prayer to be delivered from a curse:

"In the name of the Lord Jesus Christ, strengthened by the intercession of the Blessed Virgin Mary, Mother of God, of Blessed Michael the Archangel, of the Blessed Apostles Peter and Paul, and all the Saints, and powerful in the holy authority of His Precious and Wondrous Name, I ask, O Lord God, that you break and dissolve any and all curses, hexes, spells, seals, satanic vows and pacts, spiritual bondages and soul ties with satanic forces, evil wishes, evil desires, hereditary seals, snares, traps, lies, obstacles, deceptions, diversions, spiritual influences, and every dysfunction and disease from any source whatsoever, that have been placed upon me. Father in Heaven, please rebuke these evil spirits and their effects and cast them away from me so that I may continue to do Your Will and fulfil the mission You have for me to Your Greater Glory. Thank you, Father, for hearing my prayer. I praise Your Holy Name and worship you and love You. Thank You for the wisdom and light of Your Holy Spirit. Thank you for enabling me through your Holy Spirit to be aggressive against the works of the enemy. Thank you for your Hope, which takes away discouragement; thank you for ongoing victory. 'In all these things we are more than conquerors through him who loved us' (Rom. 8:37). Father, I now place my enemies into your hands. Look with mercy upon them, and do not hold their sins against them. Anyone who has cursed me, I now bless. Anyone who has hurt me, I now forgive. For those who have persecuted me, I now pray."

Our Father...
Hail Mary...
Glory Be...

Protect yourself with the word of God, which is the sword of the Spirit (cf. Eph 6:17). The following verses are very powerful when it comes to warding off the evil one. Memorise them, and recall them when the need arises. It is significant that when Jesus was tempted in the wilderness by the devil he quoted appropriate verses from the book of Deuteronomy. Here are some Bible verses that will help you to protect yourself.

- "The shield of faith puts out all the fiery darts of the evil one" (Eph 6:16). Roman soldiers had a shield that consisted of two layers of wood and was covered with leather. When their enemies were firing arrows, tipped with burning pitch, in the earlier phase of a battle, the soldiers would douse their shields with water and crouch behind them for protection. St Paul says that the shield of faith will put out *all* the fiery darts of the evil one. Scripture repeatedly makes it clear that the Lord is our spiritual shield. For example, in Prov 30:5 we read: "He (God) is a shield to those who take refuge in him" and in Ps 144:2: "He is my loving God, my fortress, my stronghold and my deliverer, my shield in whom I take refuge."
- "Submit yourselves, then, to God. Resist the devil, and he will flee from you" (Jm 4:7).
- "Your enemy the devil prowls around like a roaring lion looking for someone to devour. Resist him, standing firm in the faith" (1 Pt 5:8-9).

Take note of the verbs in the second and third quotations. Rather than being words of advice, they are words of command. Rely on God's Spirit, at work within you, to enable you to obey them (cf. Phil 2:13).

Over the years I have found that I can best express my faith by invoking the holy name of Jesus. Nestle in his protection by faith, rather than wrestling with the evil one. As Paul says in Phil 2:9-11, "at the name of Jesus every knee should bow, in heaven and on earth and under the earth, and every tongue confess that Jesus Christ is Lord, to the glory of God the Father." In other words, no matter what kind of spirit you have to contend with, when you pronounce the holy name of Jesus with faith it will protect you. Col 2:13 assures us, "having disarmed the powers and authorities, he made a public spectacle of them, triumphing over them by the cross."

Aware of the attacks of the devil, Pope Leo XIII recommended that Christians should say this prayer daily to the Archangel Michael.

"Holy Michael, the Archangel, defend us in battle. Be our safeguard against the wickedness and snares of the devil. May God rebuke him, we humbly pray; and do you, O Prince of the heavenly host, by the power of God cast into hell Satan and all the evil spirits who wander through the world seeking the ruin of souls. Amen."

If you are a Catholic pray to Mary, the Immaculate Mother of God who was full of grace. She never for a moment consented to the temptations of the evil one. As the new Eve, she is depicted crushing the head of the evil serpent with her foot. Pope Pius IX wrote:

"Just as Christ, the Mediator between God and man, assumed human nature, blotted the handwriting of the decree that stood against us, and fastened it triumphantly to the cross, so the most holy Virgin, united with him by a most intimate and indissoluble bond, was, with him and through him, eternally at enmity with the evil serpent, and most completely triumphed over him, and thus crushed his head with her immaculate foot."[128]

I can remember that on one occasion when I was praying for deliverance the Evil One spoke through the woman in a loud, guttural voice as he mocked what I was doing and claimed to have complete control over the woman. On two occasions I told the spirit to be silent, but to no effect. Then in desperation I prayed, "Mary, Im-

---

128 Apostolic Constitution *Ineffabilis Deus,* promulgating the dogma of the Immaculate Conception of the Mother of God.

maculate mother of God, help me." Immediately, the Spirit screeched, "Don't mention her, I hate her, she is too powerful with God." I was astonished. The Devil was acknowledging Mary's influence. So I continued to pray to her until the manifestations quickly ended. You too can have recourse to her. Our Lady's intercession on your behalf will be powerful with God. Say:

"O Mary conceived without sin, pray for me who have recourse to you."

Each day, make the sign of the cross, with blessed holy water and if possible wear the cross or medal of St Benedict. It is a Christian sacramental containing symbols and text related to the life of Saint Benedict of Nursia, which is used by Roman Catholics, as well as Anglicans, Lutherans, Methodists and the Western Orthodox. It is believed to be a powerful tool against evil influence which contains the following letters:

- V. R. S. (*Vade Retro Satan*): "Get away, Satan."
- N. S. M. V. (*Nunquam Suade Mihi Vana*): "Never tempt me with your vanities!"
- S. M. Q. L. (*Sunt Mala Quae Libas*): "What you offer me is evil."
- V. B. (*Ipse Venena Bibas*): "Drink the poison yourself!"

The cross can be blessed by using the following prayer.

V: Our help is in the name of the Lord

R: Who made heaven and earth.

V: In the name of God the Father + almighty, who made heaven and earth, the seas and all that is in them, I exorcise these medals against the power and attacks of the evil one.

May all who use these medals devoutly be blessed with health of soul and body. In the name of the Father + almighty, of the Son + Jesus Christ our Lord, and of the Holy + Spirit the Paraclete, and in the love of the same Lord Jesus Christ who will come on the last day to judge the living and the dead, and the world by fire.

R: Amen.

V: Let us pray. Almighty God, the boundless source of all good things, we humbly ask that, through the intercession of Saint Benedict, you pour out your blessings + upon these medals. May those who use them devoutly and earnestly strive to perform good works be blessed by you with the health of soul and body, the grace of a holy life, and remission of the temporal punishment due to sin.

May they also with the help of your merciful love, resist the temptation of the evil one and strive to exercise true charity and justice toward all, so that one day they may appear sinless and holy in your sight. This we ask through Christ our Lord.

R: Amen.

The medal is then sprinkled with holy water.

Say this prayer.

"Spirit of God, Father, Son, and Holy Spirit, most Holy Trinity, Immaculate Virgin Mary, angels, archangels, and saints of heaven, descend upon me. Please purify me, Lord, mould me, fill me with yourself, use me. Banish all the forces of evil from me, destroy them so that I can be healthy and do good deeds.

Banish from me all spells, witchcraft, black magic, harm, ties, curses, and the evil eye; diabolic infestations, oppressions, possessions; all that is evil and sinful, jealousy, envy; physical, psychological, moral, spiritual, diabolical aliments. Burn all these evils in hell, that they may never again touch me or any other creature in the entire world. I command and bid all the powers who molest me - by the power of God all powerful, in the name of Jesus Christ our Saviour, through the intercession of the Immaculate Virgin Mary - to leave me forever, and to be consigned into the everlasting hell, where they will be bound by Saint Michael the archangel, Saint Gabriel, Saint Raphael, our guardian angels, and where they will be crushed under the heel of the Immaculate Virgin Mary. Amen."

It is important to make use of the Church's sacraments because they were intended by Christ to mediate his grace to us. It is wise to attend the sacrament of reconciliation on a regular basis, e.g. monthly, and to receive the Eucharist, with faith, as often as possible. The sacrament of the anointing of the sick can help to heal traumatic wounds, which may have been exploited by the Evil One.

If a person/s has injured you in the past by deed or omission try to offer unconditional forgiveness to that person just as Jesus has repeatedly offered you his unconditional forgiveness. As St Faustina wrote, "He who knows how to forgive prepares for himself many graces from God."[129] Ask God to bring to mind anyone, living or dead who may need your forgiveness. If you have someone in mind, close your eyes. See the person standing in front of you. Notice that Jesus stands behind that person and that he loves that person as much as he loves you and that he has forgiven that person just as surely as he has forgiven you. Tell the person how you felt about the hurt or neglect they inflicted on you. Now in your heart say this prayer.

---

129 St Maria Faustina Kowalska, *Diary* (Stockbridge: Marian Press, 2015) # 390.

"Lord Jesus I thank you for forgiving all my sins even though I didn't deserve to be forgiven. You have brought to mind those who have sinned against me in the past, and who caused me a good deal of hurt. Help me, by your grace to forgive. I know that in asking for this grace I am already receiving it because I am praying within the centrality of your will. In the name of Jesus, I now forgive you from my heart for the pain you caused me. I do so without judgment or condemnation. I release you, I call down God's blessing upon you and I thank God you are now forgiven. Amen."

To forgive those who have hurt us in any way is one of the most powerful antidotes to the activity of the evil spirit because he no longer has a foothold in one's life.

When the devil reminds you of your past, remind him of his future! Say this prayer daily to put on the armour of God.

"Almighty God, today we put on the full armour to guard our lives against attack. We put on the belt of truth to protect against lies and deception. We put on the breastplate of righteousness to protect our hearts from the temptations we battle. We put the gospel of peace on our feet, so we're ready to take your light wherever you send us this day. We choose to walk in the peace and freedom of your Spirit and not be overcome with fear and anxious thoughts. We take up your shield of faith that will extinguish all the darts and threats hurled our way by the enemy. We believe in your power to protect us and choose to trust in you. We put on the helmet of salvation, which covers our minds and thoughts, reminding us we are children of the day, forgiven, set free, saved by the grace of Christ Jesus. We take up the sword of the Spirit, your very Word, the one offensive weapon given to us for battle, which has the power to demolish strongholds, alive, active, and sharper than any double-edged sword.

"We ask for your help in remembering to put on your full armour every day, for you give us all that we need to stand firm in this world. Forgive us God for the times we've been unprepared, too busy to care, or trying to fight and wrestle in our own strength.

"Thank you that we never fight alone, for you are constantly at work on our behalf, shielding, protecting, strengthening, exposing deeds of darkness, bringing to light what needs to be known, covering us from the cruel attacks we face even when we're unaware. In the powerful name of Jesus, Amen."

CONCLUSION

All of us can ward off the influence of the devil by having recourse to the guidelines described above. They are not intended to be magical. As divinely ordained means, they must be performed with faith, i.e. with firm trust that the Lord *is acting* in the present in accord with the divine promises and will. Remember what Jesus said in Mk 11:23-24, "Truly, I say to you, whoever says to this mountain, (e.g. spiritual oppression), 'Be taken up and thrown into the sea,' and *does not doubt in his heart*, but believes that what he says will come to pass, it will be done for him. Therefore I tell you, whatever you ask in prayer, believe that *you have received* it, and it will be yours."

CHAPTER TWENTY-FIVE

DELIVERANCE MINISTRY

A] SAFEGUARDING PROTOCOLS

A person who is being prayed with for deliverance should be treated as a vulnerable adult. As a result, safeguarding ethics and protocols are important. Here are some pointers. This is an area that needs attention by diocesan authorities or by the national conference of bishops.

- It is advisable to have a 'Personal Ministry Agreement Form' which states what those who are ministering deliverance are intending to do. The person being ministered to should sign the agreement form thereby indicating his or her knowing consent to that form of ministry.
- If a man is praying for a woman who needs deliverance, he should do so with the assistance of a woman or *visa versa*. Before the prayer portion of the ministry time begins, ask the petitioner if it is alright to touch them. Normally men do not need to touch women. It can facilitate transference and counter-transference which can be exploited by the adversary.
- If physical restraint is needed, it should be exercised by a person/s who have the clear permission of the person being prayed with, e.g. a woman might designate her husband, brother or trusted friend.
- Do not allow any animals to be in the room where the ministry is conducted.
- All who are involved should be bound by a confidentiality agreement.
- The exorcism should not be recorded or filmed for use afterwards.
- Explore the possibility of having those involved in the exorcism/deliverance covered by adequate insurance. I know that the Church of England recommends that the bishop

should ensure that the diocese has a policy in place to cover anyone authorised to exercise this ministry.

- Verbal language, body language and touch should be courteous and considerate. Recipients should be made aware of how the ministry is to be exercised and no one should receive any aspect of it against his or her will.

- A multi-disciplinary approach is to be desired, by consulting and collaborating as necessary with doctors, psychologists and psychiatrists, and recognising that health-care professionals are bound by professional codes of conduct.

- Ask those charged with responsibility for child safeguarding in the diocese/country what recommendations they might want to make.

- I feel that it might be a good thing to have a sheet, which would contain a list of ethical guidelines and protocols to be signed by those involved.

B] LAY PEOPLE AND SIMPLE EXORCISM

Speaking about simple exorcism or deliverance, the book *Deliverance Ministry*, says that it is the effort to free a person of the demonic oppression and bondage in Jesus' name. Deliverance, or simple exorcism, can be carried out by lay people as well as priests. St Alphonsus Liguori wrote, "Private exorcism is permissible to all Christians, solemn exorcism is permissible only to ministers who are appointed to it, and then only with the express permission of the bishop."[130] Simple exorcism does not involve a set form of prayer or liturgical rite of the Church. The term deliverance ministry is used rather than simple exorcism prayer, because this ministry is broader than prayer; it often includes bringing a person into an encounter with Jesus, helping the person bring inner wounds to light, and receive Christ's healing.

The whole subject of deliverance ministry is a big and detailed one. Those involved in this kind of ministry need to have a certain

---

130 *Theologia Moralis*, III, t 2, 492.

knowledge of abnormal psychology, e.g. dissociative identity disorder, complexes, the shadow etc., as well as an awareness of the many kinds of spiritual problems that can arise in this form of ministry, e.g. topics such as soul ties and generational curses and spells. It is not my intention to describe these conditions in this short part of the book. Suffice it to say that there are many useful books available which deal with these topics, some of which are mentioned at the end of this book.

Those who pray for deliverance need to distinguish between spiritual *oppression* and spiritual *bondage*. The former is any form of serious, continuing demonic harassment, which may be physical, e.g. the sufferings of Job, or psycho-spiritual, e.g. obsessive thoughts, irrational anxiety, self-condemnation etc. Apparently, shortly before she died, St Teresa of Calcutta, was oppressed in this way and received a simple exorcism.[131] Spiritual bondage refers to a demonic influence by which a person's will is constrained to a greater or lesser extent so that the person can no longer freely choose what is good in certain situations. While addiction may be involved, in some cases there is reason to believe that a demonic dimension is also operative. Therefore, discernment is needed, because oppression and bondage require different forms of ministry.

That is why it is important to ask him or her many questions which are intended to identify whether the presenting problem is psychological, demonic or a combination of both. Although longer questionnaires are normally used by those engaged in the ministry of deliverance, here is a brief one which is taken from the book, *Deliverance Ministry*,[132]

---

131 For more on this see P. Collins, "Mother Teresa's Dark Night of the Soul," *Doctrine and Life* (Nov. 2001), 562-566.

132 International Catholic Charismatic Renewal Services Doctrinal Commission, *Deliverance Ministry*, (Vatican City: ICCRS, 2017), 99-100. Neil Anderson's book, *Steps to Freedom in Christ* (Oxford: Monarch Book, 2009), 17-21 includes a useful "Non-Christian Spiritual Experience Inventory."

- What symptoms are you experiencing that have led you to seek deliverance or healing?
- When did they begin?
- Have you experienced any painful or traumatic events that may be linked to what you are experiencing?
- Or have you had hurtful relationships, especially in your family of origin? If so, have you forgiven the person or persons who offended you?
- Have you ever participated in any occult activity, even in seemingly innocent fun?
- Has there been any sin in your life that may also have contributed to the situation? If so, have you confessed it?
- Have you a personal relationship with the Lord?

For a longer, more comprehensive questionnaire, see Francis McNutt's *Deliverance from Evil Spirits* which contains 33 questions.[133] In his influential book *Unbound,* Neal Lozano talks about the five keys to deliverance and healing.[134] The person taking the lead in deliverance prayer can use these five keys as his or her guidelines as the oppressed person is led through them. Another person/s can act as a prayerful support.

TRY TO IDENTIFY WHAT SPIRITS ARE AT WORK

Like a good doctor who tries to diagnose what infection a patient may be contending with, those engaged in the deliverance ministry try to identify two things, are there evil spirits at work? If so, what spirits are involved? Many years ago I was asked to see a woman who claimed to be under the influence of evil spirits. Before seeing her, I talked to a Church of Ireland minister, Rev. Billy Lendrum and asked him for advice. He suggested that I interview the lady. Then he said, "when the interview is complete ask her if she would if she would

---

133 (London: Hodder & Stoughton, 1996), 172-173.
134 *Unbound: A Practical Guide to Deliverance* (Grand Rapids: Chosen, 2007), 53-118.

like you to say a prayer with her before you go your separate ways." He added, "when you pray for the woman watch what happens, see if there are any manifestations, such as speaking in a strange guttural voice. If you get that reaction, then you are probably dealing with an evil spirit." It was good advice and I followed it many times since. In the event, the woman who had been reasonable and normal throughout our conversation, suddenly became the mouthpiece of another entity. It was a clear, though not necessarily an infallible indicator, that she probably did need a deliverance.

Having established that an evil spirit/s was involved, then the question arises, what kind of spirits might they be. Francis McNutt lists four main kinds,[135]

1. Spirits of the occult: usually they have odd personal names, and are high in rank. They come from involvement with the occult. They are among the most dangerous 10%.
2. Spirits of sin, eg. lust and envy. They enter a habitation built by sin; repentance therefore is necessary.
3. Spirits of trauma. Perhaps two thirds of deliverance prayer is about this.
4. Ancestral/familiar spirits, having ordinary names. These are either demons masquerading as dead people, or souls of dead needing rest (2 theories). If in doubt, just send it to Jesus.

Neal Lozano has a helpful document on his website entitled, The Heart of the Father Ministry, under the sub-heading, "Resources". It is entitled, "Sample of Related spirits".[136]

Key 1. *Repentance and faith*. There is no greater deliverance than embracing the grace of baptism, by turning from sin and turning to the Lord. Jesus is our deliverer and He is our deliverance. The first key also involves ongoing repentance and conversion as the

135 *Deliverance from Evil Spirits*, op. cit., 170-171.
136 http://heartofthefather-dev.moja.com/files/1814/9122/7303/liestore-nounce-2.pdf

hidden sins of our heart are revealed. One way of doing this is to encourage the afflicted person to avail of the sacrament of reconciliation. Another way is to invite the person being ministered to say the miracle prayer which was mentioned above in the section on self-deliverance.

Key 2. Forgiveness. If we want to be like Jesus we need to forgive from the heart. The person being ministered to should be encouraged to forgive anyone living or dead who may have sinned against them by commission or omission. It is a good idea for the person to ask the Holy Spirit if there is any unconscious hurt that may have been repressed in the unconscious mind. As un-forgiveness, resentment and vengeful anger give the evil one a spiritual foothold, heartfelt forgiveness removes that foothold. Lead the afflicted person through a forgiveness prayer such as this, "Lord Jesus I thank you for forgiving all my sins even though I didn't deserve to be forgiven. You have brought to mind those who have sinned against me in the past, and who caused me a good deal of hurt. Help me, by your grace to forgive. I know that in asking for this grace I am already receiving it because I am praying within the centrality of your will." Then use the forgiveness in section six, point twelve above.

Key 3. Renunciation. Each Easter Catholics renew their baptismal vows beginning with, "I renounce Satan and all of his works and all of his empty promises". Renunciation is a declaration before the kingdom of darkness that the oppressed person no longer makes a home for sin, deception and the power behind it. He or she is no longer in agreement with this lie that has been active in the person's mind or heart. At this point, he or she could be encouraged to state, "I renounce fear in the name of Jesus, I renounce a spirit of rejection in the name of Jesus, I renounce lust... loneliness... a spirit of anger... resentment and bitterness... hatred. I renounce the lie that everything is my fault... I renounce the idol of fame and recognition..."

Key 4. *Command with Authority.* When the Lord said to Moses, "I will be an enemy to your enemies" (Exodus 23:22), He did not mean that Moses would sit and watch. He meant that as Moses fought, so would God. Moses had God's authority. In Christ, we too have authority over our enemies who seek to destroy us. We can take our stand against evil spirits through repentance, forgiveness, renunciation and then declaring the truth of their defeat by saying, "In the name of Jesus I command any (or every) spirit that I have renounced to leave me now."

Key 5. *Request the Father's Blessing.* The Hebrew sense of blessing means to speak words that empower someone to prosper and thrive. They are words that give life and peace. Words carry spiritual power. Every blessing that the Father spoke to Jesus is ours. The Father reveals to us who we are as we come before him in the Son. What we have longed to hear all of our lives has already been spoken. As we learn to receive His blessing, so we are healed. To be "unbound" means that the obstacles to the gift that has been waiting for us has been removed and the Father's love and affirmation is made real to us in Christ. Here is a prayer that could be said for blessing, "Father in heaven, I ask, that this brother or sister may be strengthened inwardly in his or her innermost self by the power of your Spirit that he/she may be rooted and grounded in love, and have the ability to comprehend, the length and breadth, the height and depth, of the unconditional love of Christ, which surpasses knowledge, that he/she may be filled inwardly, with the very fullness of God. Amen."

Breaking curses and spells

The Bible contains many blessings (410) and curses (230). St Paul's letters make it clear that he took curses seriously enough to ban them. In Rm 12:14 he said, "bless and do not curse". But there are malicious people who do deliberately curse other people, e.g. one of their relatives. They invoke the help of the realm of darkness in doing so.

As a result, the person who was the object of the curse may suffer mysterious forms of misfortune. In cases like these there is a need for deliverance ministry. It should be said that some curses are associated with cursed objects such as amulets, charms, or idols. Not surprisingly, The Rite of Exorcism instructs that they should be destroyed. If the ministering person has to touch them it is good that he/she would wash their hands in holy water afterwards. The following prayer can be said by the minister of deliverance to break a curse,

> "In the name of the Lord Jesus Christ of Nazareth, by the power of his cross, his blood and his resurrection, I take authority over all curses, hexes, spells, voodoo practices, witchcraft assignments, satanic rituals, incantations and evil wishes that have been sent your way, or have passed down the generational bloodline. I break their influence over your life by the power of the risen Lord Jesus Christ, and I command these curses to go back to where they came from and be replaced with a blessing."

Then ask the person being ministered to, to say the following prayer:

> "I ask forgiveness for and renounce all negative inner vows and agreements that I have made with the enemy, and I ask you Lord Jesus to release me from any bondage that may have held in me. I claim your shed blood over all aspects of my life, relationships, ministry endeavours and finances. I thank you for your enduring love, your angelic protection, and for the fullness of your abundant blessings. Amen."

Francis McNutt has a very helpful chapter entitled, "Falling under a Curse," in his book *Deliverance from Evil Spirits: A Practical Manual*. Not only does he describe different types of curse, he also indicates how they can be overcome.[137] The late Fr Rufus Pereira, an Indian

---

137   (London: Hodder & Stoughton, 1996), 101-125.

exorcist I knew, said that when it came to spells he would say, "In the name of Jesus I break the spell that has been cast upon you and every member of your family." Then he would pray in tongues and things would happen. He said that he never came across a single case where the spell was not broken when he employed this approach.

DEMONIC MANIFESTATIONS

Those who pray for deliverance are familiar with manifestations that are sometimes associated with the evil spirit's presence.

- Unnatural physical strength.
- Knowledge of hidden things, e.g. facts about a person's past life.
- Speaking languages that the oppressed person doesn't know.
- Blasphemous rejection of sacred things, e.g. the Eucharist and holy water.
- A common one is the phenomenon of the spirit seeming to speak through his victim in a guttural voice, which is quite unlike the person's normal voice. Typically, it will mock the person who is praying while asserting the devil's authority over the oppressed person.
- On other occasions the person may foam at the mouth or writhe on the ground or lapse into a trance like state.
- Sometimes there will be a bad smell or odour.

I have found that it is important not to focus on the distracting activity of the devil, but rather to keep one's attention firmly fixed on Jesus and on the person who is being prayed with. One does so in the belief that "the Spirit who lives in you is greater than the spirit who lives in the world" (1 Jn 4:4). I have also found that it is good to encourage the person receiving ministry to fight against lapsing into a trance and to use their will power to call on Jesus for help. I can remember praying with others for a woman. Although she was writhing on the floor and foaming at the mouth, she did cooperate with those who were praying for her by calling out the name of Jesus for help. Eventually, thank God, she became peaceful.

TWO FORMS OF PRAYER

Two forms of prayer are involved in deliverance ministry.

Firstly, there are prayers of supplication asking God for a particular grace. For instance, St Vincent Ferrer recommended the following simple prayer, "These signs shall follow those that believe: 'In My Name they shall cast out devils.' May Jesus, the Son of Mary, the Saviour and Master of the world, who has brought you to the Catholic faith, preserve you within it, and make you blessed, and graciously grant to deliver your body from the devil. Amen."[138]

Secondly, there are prayers of command in the name of God or Jesus. In the context of deliverance it is a command addressed to the evil spirits to leave the afflicted person.

The book *Deliverance Ministry*, which was mentioned above, says "Church teaching contains clear warnings against any form of conversation with demons, including asking them questions, seeking information from them, or asking them for favours. Our only interactions with demons should be simple commands to bind, silence, or expel them." In saying this it is echoing what Cardinal Ratzinger said in a letter on exorcism in 1985. That said, of course, the person praying for deliverance can ask the Holy Spirit to reveal the identity of evil spirits to be expelled, e.g. through a word of knowledge or the gift of discernment of spirits.

---

138 Andrew Pradel, O.P., *St. Vincent Ferrer, O.P., The Order of Friar Preachers: His Life, Spiritual Teaching, & Practical Devotion* (London: Washbourne, 1875), 223.

CHAPTER TWENTY-SIX

GUIDELINES FOR PRAYING FOR DELIVERANCE

The United States Conference of Catholic Bishops has an excellent section on its website entitled, Frequently Asked Questions about Exorcism, which is well worth reading.[139] At this point I would like to include some guidelines which have helped me and others when praying for deliverance.

Begin with the following prayer for protection which was written by Dr Francis McNutt.

"In the name of Jesus Christ and by the power of his Cross and his Blood, we bind up the power of any evil spirits and command them not to block our prayers. We break any curses, hexes or spells sent against us and declare them null and void. We break the assignments of any spirits sent against us and send them to Jesus to deal with them as he will. Lord, we ask you to bless our enemies by sending your Holy Spirit to lead them to repentance and conversion. Furthermore, we bind all interaction and communication in the world of evil spirits as it affects us and our ministry. We ask for the protection of the shed blood of Jesus Christ over you. (mention the person's name). Thank you, Lord, for your protection and send your angels, especially St Michael, the Archangel, to help us in the battle. We ask you to guide us in our prayers: share with us your Spirit's power and compassion. Amen."

While we talk about God and the Devil, good and evil, there is no equivalence between them. God is the all-powerful creator of all that exists, while the devil, though powerful, is merely a creature.

---

139 http://www.usccb.org/prayer-and-worship/sacraments-and-sacramentals/sacramentals-blessings/exorcism.cfm

That was obvious in the exorcisms of Jesus who repeatedly liberated people from the oppression of the Evil One.

Jesus won a definitive victory over the Devil by means of his saving death and resurrection. As a result, as the author of Col 2:14 asserts, he "disarmed the powers and authorities, he made a public spectacle of them, triumphing over them by the cross". When we pray for deliverance, we claim in practice what is already true in principle.

Jesus promised us as believers, "Very truly I tell you, whoever believes in me will do the works I have been doing" (Jn 14:12). Paul said much the same in Phil 2:13, "For God is working in you, giving you the desire and the power to do what pleases him." Par 521 of the *Catechism of the Catholic Church*, echoes those points when it says, "Christ enables us to live in him *all* that he himself lived and he lives it in us." Christ was an exorcist and he continues his ministry in and through his disciples.

Knowing this to be true I often say the following prayer before engaging in deliverance ministry:

"Lord Jesus, the good I wish to do, I cannot do, but you are living out the mysteries of your life in me. Enable me, by the Spirit that animated your life of generous service, to continue and fulfil your mission in my life. Give me the ability to pray effectively for deliverance for this person, and I thank you, that you will enable me achieve even more than I can ask, or think, through the power of your Spirit at work within me. Amen."

When we pray for physical healing, we cannot always be sure that we are always praying within the will of God for this particular person at a particular time. But it is always within God's will that we pray for deliverance from evil spirits. So we can pray with expectant faith because as 1 Jn 5:14-15 states, "This is the confidence we have in approaching God: that if we ask anything according to his will, he hears us. And if we know that he hears us, we know that *we have* [present tense] what we asked of him". Notice what St John says.

As soon as a priest or lay person prays for deliverance, he or she can be sure that straight away the request or command begins to be responded to by God. That is why St Paul could say in Phil 4:6, "by prayer and petition, with *thanksgiving* [anticipatory gratitude] present your requests to God."

In 2 Cor 10:4-5 St Paul stated, "For the weapons of our warfare are not of the flesh but have divine power to destroy strongholds. We destroy arguments and every lofty opinion raised against the knowledge of God, and take every thought captive to obey Christ." As was mentioned already, the strongholds Paul talks about are forms of thinking and feeling that are being influenced by the Evil Spirit either in the form of bondage or oppression. But Paul says that those who are engaged in deliverance prayer have the power to tear down those strongholds. As 1 Jn 4:4, assures us, "the one who is in you [the Holy Spirit] is greater than the one who is in the world [Satan]". Of course, one needs to identify firstly, what those strongholds are and secondly, how and when the Evil One got a foothold in the person's life. In chapter twenty-three we looked at nine possibilities and in chapter twenty-five we included some pertinent questions. The pre-ministry is important in that regard, as is prayer for the gift of discernment of spirits, e.g. by means of a word of knowledge, during the time of ministry. Good diagnosis leads to focused, effective prayer. It is good to keep checking in with the person being prayed with to find out what they think and how they feel. Try to get the person to fight against trance-like states while encouraging him or her to resist the evil one, e.g. by saying the name of Jesus repeatedly.

I think that Neal Losano is right when he says that one should focus on Jesus and the person, rather than on the Evil Spirit. Don't ask the Devil any questions, e.g. his name. Do not focus on distracting manifestations, such as guttural utterances of a defiant kind. Help the person being prayed with to renounce any strongholds he or she is aware of while commanding them to crumble and leave. The person praying can also utter such a command. Faith rather than loudness of voice is what is important at this point.

Because the Evil One can exploit an afflicted person's emotional wounds, it may be necessary to pray for inner healing, and healing of memories. As St Paul says, in Eph 3:16-19, "I pray that out of his glorious riches he may strengthen you with power through his Spirit in your inner being, so that Christ may dwell in your hearts through faith. And I pray that you, being rooted and established in love, may have power, together with all the Lord's holy people, to grasp how wide and long and high and deep is the love of Christ, and to know this love that surpasses knowledge - that you may be filled to the measure of all the fullness of God." When the prayer is completed the person could be encouraged to seek counselling or psychotherapy for further healing of their inner wounds and traumas.

One can use a St Benedict's cross, during the prayer. The late Fr Sean Conaty, an exorcist in the Diocese of Hexam and Newcastle told me that the devil hates a wooden cross, as a result I use a wooden St Benedict's crucifix. For example, the person being prayed with could hold it, while looking at it with faith. Blessed holy water can also be used to good effect. Many of the points mentioned in chapter twenty-four may be relevant when ministering to another person, e.g. having recourse to Our Lady of the Immaculate Conception.

It is good to say a prayer to block spirit transference. Something like the following words could be used.

"In the name of Jesus Christ, I forbid and block all satanic and demonic activities from transferring to me, any of my family or into our lives. I ask you Father God, in the name of Jesus Christ, to surround myself, family, community, church, leaders and colleagues from warring angels. The blood of Jesus be between us and the forces of hell. Amen."

Having engaged in deliverance ministry there is no need to be afraid. As Origen, a 3rd Century Church Father wrote, "Christians have nothing to fear, even if demons should not be well disposed to them; for they are protected by the supreme God, who is well pleased with their piety, and who sets his divine angels to watch over those who are worthy of such guardianship, so that they can suffer nothing from demons. As Ps 27:1 says, 'The Lord is my light and my salvation; whom shall I fear? The Lord is the strength of my life; of whom shall I be afraid? Though an host should encamp against me, my heart shall not fear'.'

Over the years I have found that deliverance prayer may have to be repeated many times, sometimes over a period of years, before the afflicted person is completely freed of demonic influence. I was interested to see that the late Fr Gabriele Amorth, a famous Italian exorcist, made that point in his books, which are mentioned in the bibliography below. Psychotherapist Norberto R. Keppe says something similar. Having quoted the following observation by Fr Amorth, "It takes many years to liberate the possessed", he goes on to say, "in practical terms, this is exactly the same as psychotherapy where it takes some time in treatment for the neurotic person to improve his life. What is even more significant, however, is the astonishing similarity we find between physical and spiritual illness when we compare the behaviour of mentally ill and demonically possessed individuals."[140] One possible reason why this may be so is the fact that exorcism is a sacramental and not a sacrament. Furthermore, the devil is a master of deception, who will hide during a deliverance prayer, only to reappear.

A question that is often asked is, how does one know that the evil spirits have departed? Francis McNutt suggests that there are three reliable ways.[141] Firstly, there is the judgment of the prayer team by means of the gift of the discernment of spirits. It may be that, yes indeed, the spirit you were praying against has left but others remain. They would need to be tackled, perhaps at another time. In those cases, say a prayer commending the person to the care of God while commanding the evil spirit not to disturb the person. Secondly, the man or woman being prayed with will often have a sense whether the spirit/s is gone. He or she might say, "It's gone, I feel so much lighter now." Thirdly, it is a matter of human observation, e.g. the person may

140 *Psychotherapy and Exorcism*, op. cit., 26.
141 *Deliverance from Evil Spirits*, op. cit., 188-190.

cough a retching cough as the spirit leaves. There can also be scream-ing which fades away. Again, one can confirm what is happening by asking the person how he or she is feeling.

CONCLUSION

I would have to say that deliverance ministry is characterised by all kinds of difficult situations which I have not mentioned here, e.g. what do you do if the person being ministered to either won't or can't speak? The devil is a liar, so you can take it for granted that the devil will use all kinds of deceptions to distract those who are ministering. That is where those who are praying need to be tuned in to the in-spirations of the Holy Spirit. Often the person who is oppressed will lapse into a sort of trance during the time of ministry.

As the time of ministry ends, those on the deliverance could say this precautionary prayer.

"Lord Jesus, thank you for sharing with us your wonderful ministry of healing and deliverance. Thank you for the heal-ings we have seen and experienced today. But we realise that the sickness and evil we encounter is more than our humanity can bear. So cleanse us of any sadness, negativity or despair that we may have picked up. If our ministry has tempted me to anger, impatience or lust, cleanse us of those tempta-tions and replace them with love, joy and peace. If any evil spirits have attached themselves to us or oppress us in any way, we command you, spirits of earth, air, fire or water, of the netherworld or of nature, to depart now and go straight to Jesus Christ, for him to deal with as he will. Come Holy Spirit, renew us, fill us anew with your power, life and joy. Strengthen us where we have felt weak and clothe us with your light. Fill us with life. And Lord Jesus, please send your holy angels to minister to our families, and us, and to guard and protect us from all sickness, harm and accidents, and guard us on a safe trip home. I praise you now and forever, Father, Son and Holy Spirit!"

Finally, as was already mentioned, all kinds of psychological traumas, hurting memories and emotional wounds can afford the evil one a foothold in a person's life. In those cases, it is important not only to pray for deliverance, there may also be a need afterwards for inner healing which could be facilitated by seeing a counsellor or therapist as well as being prayed with for healing of memories. There are many excellent books available on the subject of inner healing such as *Inner Healing: Ministering to the Human Spirit Through the Power of Prayer* by the late Michael Scanlon, TOR[142] and *Healing Prayer: Spiritual Pathways to Health and Wellness*[143] and *Healing the Hidden Self*[144] by Barbara Shlemon Ryan. Inner healing is important because if it is overlooked, the evil one could exploit the hurts again.

---

142 (New York: Paulist, 1974).
143 (Ventura CA: Vine Books, 2001).
144 (Ann Arbor: Ave Maria Press, 2005).

CHAPTER TWENTY-SEVEN

CLEANSING DISTURBED BUILDINGS

Over the years I have been contacted by people who say that places such as their house, place of work or farm is haunted or cursed. They will talk about hearing sounds, seeing strange and frightening images, becoming aware of a foul smell, cattle dying mysteriously etc. If one rules out purely physical and psychological reasons for phenomena like this, such as an over excited imagination as a result of deep-seated fears, misinterpreting sounds and shadows, drinking too much alcohol, taking drugs, and watching horror movies, there are two possible explanations.

A] *HUMAN SPIRIT HAUNTING*

Firstly, there is reason to think that the spirit of a dead person, who is in purgatory, may continue to be associated with a particular place. He or she may be reluctant to leave it because of unfinished business. So he or she haunts the area they were familiar with during life. Adam C. Blai says in 'Human spirit haunting', "Some of the typical indications that a human soul in purgatory may be present are sounds of a person walking or pacing, odours that were associated with that person, knocks on the walls, and in cases of suicide a heavy and sad feeling in the area where the suicide occurred. There is almost always a lack of speech on the part of these souls."[145]

If I'm consulted about a haunting, I encourage the people in the disturbed house or building to try and find out who the disturbed soul might be. Sometimes discrete enquiries in the neighbourhood lead to relevant information. In my experience, it is often about someone who suffered some kind of injustice, violence or trauma in that location. For example, I visited one house where the whimper of a baby was often heard. Then by chance the family heard that a baby had

---

145 *Possession, Exorcism, and Hauntings*, (GB: Amazon, 2014), 46.

been abused there, many years before they bought the house. The restless spirit may give the impression of being playful, resentful or angry. One can pray in the house, urging the restless soul to move on to meet with a loving and merciful God. It might be good to pray, if need be, that the Lord would forgive the perpetrator for his or her wrongdoing. Adam C. Blai recommends that the Office of the Dead be prayed in the house. A requiem Mass could also be said in the place in order to commend the restless spirit/s of the dead to the mercy and love of God.

A question I keep in mind when interviewing a householder/s who lives in a 'haunted' house, is this, "If you leave the house for a time, e.g. to go on holiday, do you still experience the problem?" If they answer yes, it is probable that the spirit, whether human or demonic, is associated with the person rather than the place and therefore that he or she would need appropriate forms of ministry. I have heard it said that some disturbances are paranormal, and not necessarily associated with spirits of any kind. To say something is paranormal means that it is natural although at present the phenomenon isn't amenable to a verifiable scientific explanation. For example, it has been suggested that some poltergeist (noisy spirit) activity may be caused by the psychic energy of the person in the place. Apparently, there is circumstantial evidence, which suggests that some poltergeist activity may be activated by adolescent women just at the beginning of their periods.

B] DEMONIC INFESTATION

Secondly, a house can be a place where demons gain the right to manifest their presence. In chapters entitled, 'Demonic Infestation' and 'Resolving Demonic Infestation', Adam C. Blai describes some common causes and signs why demonic spirits may be present.[146] In his book, *Demons, Deliverance and Discernment*, Mike Driscoll writes, "What is certain is that demons can cause the things we commonly associate with haunted houses. They can make noises and move

---

146 Ibid, 49-54.

objects; they can trigger air movements, such as a breeze; and they can cause the temperature in a room to drop. Demons can appear in the form of human beings, including someone who once lived in the haunted house, or even our own family members and friends."[147] It is clear, therefore, that discernment is needed. The question is whether the disturbance in the house is due to human or evil spirits. In his book, *Deliverance from Evil Spirits*, Francis McNutt says that deliverance prayer is needed in rooms, and buildings under the following circumstances:[148]

- When they have been targeted by curses, hexes, and spells by evil-minded groups
- When crimes or other serious sins have been committed there
- When people infested by evil spirits have lived or spent time visiting a place. I found that when I visited a disturbed house in the North of Ireland in the company of an exorcist from the Church of Ireland, we finally came to the conclusion, following some historical research, that a crime had been committed in that place long before the house had been built. I can remember having to pray a prayer of exorcism in order to cleanse the place. As I did so the owner of the house wanted to vomit. As he rushed out the door into the back garden he felt that his back had been burnt. When his shirt was raised there was a red welt across his back.

When there is reason to believe that an evil spirit is involved a priest exorcist needs to be contacted. He could say a prayer like the following:

"I bind every evil spirit that is in this room and command them to flee right now and go where Jesus Christ sends them. I renounce and reject any inch of this house and property that has been yielded or surrendered to Satan and by faith I

---

147 (El Cajon, Calif: Catholic Answers, 2015), 52.
148 (London: Hodder & Stoughton, 1996), 288-289.

take it back and surrender it to the Lord Jesus Christ. By faith, I claim that this room is covered by the blood of the Lord Jesus Christ and no evil spirit can enter it." (Pray this in every room in the house) After going through every room in the house pray, "I dedicate and consecrate this home to the Lord Jesus Christ and Satan has no hold on it at all. I surrender everything in this house to the Lord Jesus Christ and claim it is under his divine protection including all electrical wiring and plumbing. I bind every evil spirit that is in this house by the precious blood of the lamb and command them to flee and go where the Lord Jesus Christ sends them. I claim by faith that everything in this house is covered by the blood of Jesus Christ from the top of the roof to the foundations below and everything in between and especially anything that conducts electricity. I claim by faith that this house is surrounded by a hedge of perfection, a wall of fire, a wall of faith, and covered by the blood of the Lord Jesus Christ on all sides, above and below. I pray that powerful warring angels would come to protect the four corners of this house and property and everyone inside. Thank you for the complete victory we already have in Jesus Christ. I ask that this home be consecrated by your divine presence so that everyone who enters it will be blessed with spiritual blessings from heavenly places. Amen."

Another prayer that can be said in a haunted house, particularly if there is reason to believe that evil spirits have influenced the place, is the Prayer of Simple Exorcism to St Michael which was written by Pope Leo XIII. Church authorities have made it clear that it should only be said by a priest. It is officially entitled, the *Exorcism of Satan and the Fallen Angels*. It can be found at the end of this section. The 1999 Rite of Exorcism entitled, *Exorcism and Certain Supplications* also contains prayers for this purpose in appendix one entitled, 'A Supplication and Exorcism which May be Used in Particular Circumstances of the Church'.

In an article entitled, "Exorcism and Prayers for Deliverance: The Position of the Catholic Church," Dr Gareth Leyshon, a priest of the Archdiocese of Cardiff has written, "It should not be forgotten that simpler remedies – such as blessing the place with holy water (perhaps exorcised using the older Roman Ritual) – or celebrating Mass in the place – may have a powerful effect without needing to have recourse to the Rite of Exorcism. The inhabitants of a place may, of course, make free private use of the prayers in Appendix II of *Exorcism and Certain Supplications*. It is available for sale in booklet form with the title, *Prayers against the Powers of Darkness*, on the website of the American bishops. My colleague, William H. Lendrum wrote about cleansing disturbed buildings in his *Confronting the Paranormal: A Christian Perspective* (Belfast: Divine Healing Ministries), 95-102."

CHAPTER TWENTY-EIGHT

SOLEMN EXORCISM

On the website of the United States Conference of Catholic Bishops there is a section that deals with the exorcism of people who are deemed to be possessed. It is a matter of the inner control by the devil of the actions of the body of a human being. The victim's liberty of soul always remains intact. Possession can be continual or intermittent, and the victim need not have culpably brought on the devil's control. A question arises, may anyone receive a 'major exorcism'? In reply the bishops say that, firstly, the rite of solemn exorcism is categorised not as a sacrament but as a sacramental. Secondly, the determination of who may receive a 'major exorcism' is governed by canon 1170 of the *Code of Canon Law*. The following are able to receive this ecclesiastical blessing if it is determined necessary:

- Catholics
- Catechumens
- Non-Catholic Christians who request it
- Non-Christians provided they have the proper disposition— meaning, they are sincere in their desire to be free of demonic influence. In cases involving a non-Catholic, the matter should be brought to the attention of the diocesan bishop. I am told that nowadays quite a number of Muslims are asking Christians for exorcism.

On rare occasions a person ministering to someone who feels oppressed by evil spirits will come to the conclusion that he or she is possessed and in need of solemn exorcism. The American bishops say that, "As part of the evaluation process (which can be established in a diocesan protocol), the afflicted member of the faithful should avail himself or herself of a thorough medical and psychological or psychiatric evaluation." I think it would not only be wise for bishops to insist on such an examination they should also ask for a written report. It can be important to remember that more often than not those who seem to be in need of a solemn exorcism are in fact mentally ill. That said, it is remotely possible of course, that someone who is mentally ill could also be possessed.

Frequently, individuals present themselves claiming to be afflicted in any number of ways. Historically, however, the Church has exercised caution when evaluating such individuals for fear of unnecessarily drawing attention to the activities of the devil or giving credit where no credit is due. In par. 16 of *Exorcisms and Certain Supplications* (1999), some of the typical symptoms of possession are listed as:

- Speaking a number of words in a language unknown to the afflicted person
- Understanding someone speaking an unknown language
- Making known distant and hidden events
- Possessing strength beyond the person's age or condition

Such signs can offer some indication. Since however, signs of this kind are not necessarily to be reckoned as coming from the devil, it is also necessary to pay attention to other things, especially those of the moral and spiritual order which in another way manifest diabolical intervention, as for example, vehement aversion from God, the most holy name of Jesus, the blessed Virgin Mary and the saints, the Church, the word of God, sacred things and rites, especially sacramental ones, and from sacred images.

If there is good reason to believe that a person does need a solemn exorcism, Cardinal Suenens has made the important observation in his book, *Renewal and the Powers of Darkness,* that, "All theologians agree that the Devil cannot penetrate into the intimate depths of the soul unless the subject voluntarily surrenders them to him."[149] That being so, it is prudent to try to identify when and how that surrender took place.

---

149 (London: Darton: Longman & Todd, 1980), 31.

When a person is deemed to be in need of a solemn exorcism, it can only be performed by a priest who has been appointed by the bishop in that diocese. As canon 1172 of the *Code of Canon Law* states, "No one can perform exorcisms legitimately upon the possessed unless he has obtained special and express permission from the local ordinary. The local ordinary is to give this permission only to a presbyter who has piety, knowledge, prudence, and integrity of life." Par. 1673 of the *Catechism of the Catholic Church* says, "The solemn exorcism, called 'a major exorcism', can be performed only by a priest and with the permission of the bishop. The priest must proceed with prudence, strictly observing the rules established by the Church. Exorcism is directed at the expulsion of demons or to the liberation from demonic possession through the spiritual authority which Jesus entrusted to his Church." Priest exorcists can purchase the English translation of the Rite of Exorcism from the publishing wing of the United States Conference of Catholic Bishops. It should be said that following criticisms by the late Fr Amorth, the chief exorcist of Rome, many exorcists feel that the modern rite, which was published in 1999, is defective, so they continue to use the old 1614 version.

The Church recommends that solemn exorcisms be conducted in a sacred space such as a chapel or an oratory. The priest exorcist should be suitably dressed with a stole. If at all possible and appropriate, a priest exorcist can be assisted by other clergy and/or mature lay people. Although they do not perform the exorcism, they support the exorcist and the person being ministered to by means of their love and fervent prayer together with any practical help that may be needed.

It is important to establish whether a person who has received a solemn exorcism has been truly delivered from the influence of the evil spirit/s or not. Anyone who has engaged in this form of ministry knows that the devil is subtle and deceptive. He will conceal himself and leave the person almost free from any physical disturbance so that the victim may believe the he or she has been completely freed. But the exorcist should not stop until he sees the sure signs of deliverance. As Mike Driscoll says, "Demons may shriek when they are driven out and the possessed individuals themselves may have a sense of their departure. Sometimes there is a noticeable peculiar exhaling from the nose and/or mouth that accompanies the exodus of the demons."

When a person has been freed from demonic influence, par. 36 of *Exorcisms and Certain Supplications* says, "It is desirable that the faithful person, after being freed from torment should render thanks to God for the peace received, either alone or in company with close friends. Moreover, the person should be led to persevere in prayer, drawing it most especially from Sacred Scripture, and to frequent the sacraments of reconciliation and the Eucharist and also to lead a Christian life full of works of charity and fraternal love towards all." For a more extended discussion of solemn exorcism, see Fr Mike Driscoll, 'The Rite of Exorcism', in *Demons, Deliverance, and Discernment*.[150]

In the unlikely event that you know a person who may need a solemn exorcism, talk to your parish priest and ask him to contact the bishop on your behalf to see if any trained exorcist is available to assess the situation and to arrange, if necessary, to conduct the rite. Unfortunately, there are still many dioceses in Ireland which do not have a trained exorcist who can help an afflicted person to discern, not only whether a solemn exorcism is needed, but also how to carry it out.

Conclusion

Nobel-prize-winner Bob Dylan wrote songs which contained the words, "You're gonna have to serve somebody, Well, it may be the devil or it may be the Lord, But you're gonna have to serve somebody... there ain't no neutral ground." Those lyrics reflect the New Testament worldview which sees life as a spiritual combat, a battle between good and evil spirits. Well-known Catholic scripture scholar, John Meier, confirmed this worldview when he wrote in his book *A Marginal Jew*, Vol. II, *Mentor, Message & Miracles*, "It is important to realise that, in the view of Jesus... human beings were not basically neutral territories that might be influenced by divine or demoic forces

---

150   (El Cajon, AA: Catholic Answers Press, 2015), 76-90.

now and then... Human existence was seen as a battlefield dominated by one or the other supernatural force, God or Satan (alias Belial or the devil). A human being might have a part in choosing which 'field of force' would dominate his or her life, i.e. which force he or she would choose to side with. But no human being was free to choose simply to be free of these supernatural forces. One was dominated by either one or the other, and to pass *from* one was necessarily to pass *into* the control of the other. At least over the long term, one could not maintain a neutral stance *vis-a-vis* God and Satan."[151] In the words of St Peter, "as servants of God, live as free people, yet do not use your freedom as a pretext for evil" (1 Pt 2:16-17). Hopefully, this brief introductory treatment will help readers to journey on the road less travelled which leads to both spiritual freedom in this life and eternal glory in the next.

---

151   (New York: Yale University Press, 1994),415.

CHAPTER TWENTY-NINE

SOME RECOMMENDED PRAYERS & CHURCH NORMS

A] Prayer of Simple Exorcism to St Michael by Pope Leo XIII

+ In the Name of the Father, and of the Son, and of the Holy Spirit. Amen.

Most glorious Prince of the heavenly host, Saint Michael the Archangel, defend us in the conflict which we have to sustain against principalities and powers, against the rulers of the world of this darkness, against the spirits of wickedness in the high places (Eph. 6.12). Come to the rescue of people who God has created in His image and likeness, and who He has redeemed at a great price from the tyranny of the devil. It is you whom Holy Church venerates as her guardian and protector; you who the Lord has charged to conduct redeemed souls into Heaven. Pray, therefore, that God of Peace to subdue Satan beneath our feet, that he may no longer retain men captive nor do injury to the Church. Present our prayers to the most High, that without delay they may draw His mercy down upon us. Seize the dragon, the old serpent, which is the devil and Satan, bind him and cast him into the bottomless pit, that he may no more seduce the nations (Apoc. 20.2-3).

Exorcism

In the name of Jesus Christ, our Lord and Saviour, strengthened by the intercession of the Immaculate Virgin Mary, Mother of God, of Blessed Michael the Archangel, of the Blessed Apostles Peter and Paul, and all the Saints, and powerful in the holy authority of our ministry, we confidently undertake to repulse the attacks and deceits of the devil.

PSALM 67

Let God arise, and let His enemies be scattered: and let those who hate Him flee from before His face.

As smoke vanishes, so let them vanish away: as wax melts before the fire, so let the wicked perish at the presence of God.

V. Behold the Cross of the Lord! Flee, bands of enemies.

R. The Lion of the tribe of Juda, the offspring of David has conquered.

V. May Your mercy descend upon us.

R. As great as our hope is in You.

We drive you from us, whoever you may be, unclean spirits, Satanic powers, infernal invaders, wicked legions, assemblies, and sects. In the name and by the virtue of Our Lord Jesus Christ +. May you be snatched away and driven from the Church of God and from the souls redeemed by the Precious Blood of the Divine Lamb +.

Cease audacious, cunning serpent, to deceive the human race, to persecute the Church, to torment God's elect, and to sift them as wheat +. This is the command made to you by the Most High God +, with Whom in your haughty insolence you still pretend to be equal +. The God Who wills that all people be saved, and to come to the knowledge of the truth (I Tim. 2.4). God the Father commands you +. God the Son commands you +. God the Holy Spirit commands you +. Christ, the Eternal Word of God made Flesh, commands you +. He Who to save our race, outdone through your malice, humbled Himself, becoming obedient unto death (Phil. 2.8). He Who has built His Church on the firm rock and declared that the gates of hell shall not prevail against Her, because He dwells with Her all days, even to the consummation of the world (Matt. 28.20). The hidden virtue of the Cross requires it of you, as does the power of the mysteries of the Christian Faith +. The glorious Mother of God, the Virgin Mary, commands you +. She who by Her humility and from the first moment of Her Immaculate

Conception crushed your proud head. The faith of the holy Apostles Peter and Paul and of the other Apostles commands you +. The blood of the Martyrs and the pious intercession of all the Saints command you +.

Thus, cursed dragon, and you, wicked legions, we command you by the living God +, by the true God +, by the holy God +, by the God Who so loved the world, as to give up His only-begotten Son that whosoever believes in Him may not perish but may have life everlasting (St John 3.16). Cease deceiving human creatures and pouring out to them the poison of eternal perdition. Cease harming the Church and hindering her liberty. Retreat, Satan, inventor and master of all deceit, enemy of man's salvation. Cede the place to Christ in Whom you have found none of your works. Cede the place to the One, Holy, Catholic, and Apostolic Church acquired by Christ at the price of His Blood. Bend low beneath the all-powerful Hand of God. Tremble and flee at the evocation of the Holy and terrible name of Jesus; this Name which causes hell to tremble; this Name to which the Virtues, Powers and Dominations of Heaven are humbly submissive; this Name which the Cherubim and Seraphim praise unceasingly, repeating: Holy, Holy, Holy is the Lord, the God of Hosts.

V. O Lord hear my prayer.

R. And let my cry come unto You.

V. The Lord be with you

R. And with your spirit.

LET US PRAY.

God of Heaven, God of earth, God of Angels, God of Archangels, God of Patriarchs, God of Prophets, God of Apostles, God of Martyrs, God of Confessors, God of Virgins, God who has power to give life after death and rest after work, because there is no other God than You and there can be no other, for You are the Creator of all things, visible and invisible, of Whose reign there shall be no end. We humbly prostrate ourselves before Your glorious Majesty and we implore You to deliver us from all the tyranny of the infernal spirits, from their snares, their lies, and their furious wickedness. Grant O Lord, to protect us by Your power and to preserve us safe and sound. We beseech You through Jesus Christ Our Lord. Amen.

V. From the snares of the devil,

R. Deliver us, O Lord.

V. That Your Church may serve You in peace and liberty,

R. We beseech You to hear us.

V. That You would crush down all enemies of Thy Church,

R. We beseech You to hear us.

(Holy water is sprinkled in the place where we may be.)

St Michael the Archangel, defend us in battle, be our protection against the wickedness and snares of the devil. May God rebuke him, we humbly pray. O Prince of the Heavenly Host, by the Divine Power of God, cast into hell Satan and all the evil spirits who wander throughout the world seeking the ruin of souls. Amen.

B] Five Prayers from Appendix II of *Exorcism and Certain Supplications*

(These prayers can be used by lay people)

Have mercy, Lord God, on me your servant, who have become like a vessel that is lost because of the host that besieges me. Snatch me from the hands of my enemies and draw near to me, that you may seek what is lost, restore to yourself what is found and not abandon what is restored; so that in all things I may be pleasing to you, by whom I know I have been powerfully redeemed. Through Christ our Lord. Amen.

Almighty God, who give the forsaken a home to live in and lead captives into prosperity look upon my affliction and rise up to help me. Strike down the most wicked foe, so that, after the enemy is driven away, freedom may bring me peace. And so, restored to tranquil devotion, may I confess how wonderful you are, who have given power to your people. Through Christ our Lord. Amen.

God, creator and defender of the human race, who formed man in your own image and more wonderfully recreated him by the grace of baptism, look with favour upon me, your servant, and graciously hear my prayers. May the splendour of your glory dawn in my heart, I pray, so that with all terror, fear and dread removed, and serene in mind and spirit, I may be able to praise you with my brothers and sisters in your Church. Through Christ our Lord. Amen.

God. Author of every mercy and all goodness, who willed your Son to submit for our sake to the yoke of the Cross, so that you might drive from us the power of the enemy, look with mercy upon my lowliness and pain, and grant, I pray, that defeating the onslaught of the Evil One, you will fill with the grace of your blessing the one you made new in the font of baptism. Through Christ our Lord. Amen.

God, who through the grace of adoption chose me to be a child of light, grant I pray, that I may not be shrouded in the darkness of demons, but always be seen to stand in the bright light of the freedom that I have received from you. Through Christ our Lord. Amen.

C] ANCIENT PRAYERS FOR SALT AND WATER FOR USE IN DELIVERANCE

"God's creature, salt, I cast out the demon from you by the living God, by the true God, by the holy God, by God who ordered you to be thrown into the water-springs by Elisha to heal it of its barrenness. May you be a purified salt, a means of health for those who believe, a medicine for body and soul for all who make use of you. May all evil fancies of the foul fiend, his malice and cunning, be driven afar from the place where you are sprinkled. And let every unclean spirit be repulsed by him who is coming to judge both the living and the dead and the world by fire. Amen. Let us pray. Almighty everlasting God, we humbly appeal to your mercy and goodness to graciously bless this creature, salt, which you have given for mankind's use. May all who use it find in it a remedy for body and mind. And may everything that it touches or sprinkles be freed from uncleanness and any influence of the evil spirit; through Christ our Lord. Amen."

"May you be a purified water, empowered to drive afar all power of the enemy, in fact, to root out and banish the enemy himself, along with his fallen angels. We ask this through the power of our Lord Jesus Christ... May everything that this water sprinkles in the homes and gatherings of the faithful be delivered from all that is unclean and hurtful; let no breath of contagion hover there, no taint of corruption; let all the wiles of the lurking enemy come to nothing. By the sprinkling of this water may everything be opposed to the safety and peace of the occupants of these homes be banished, so that in calling on your holy name they may know the well-being they desire, and be protected from every period; through Christ our Lord. Amen."

D] Letter to Ordinaries regarding norms on Exorcism

"Recent years have seen an increase in the number of prayer groups in the Church aimed at seeking deliverance from the influence of demons, while not actually engaging in real exorcisms. These meetings are led by lay people, even when a priest is present.

"As the Congregation for the Doctrine of the Faith has been asked how one should view these facts, this Dicastery considers it necessary to inform bishops of the following response:

Canon 1172 of the Code of Canon Law states that no one can legitimately perform exorcisms over the possessed unless he has obtained special and express permission from the local Ordinary (§ 1), and states that this permission should be granted by the local Ordinary only to priests who are endowed with piety, knowledge, prudence and integrity of life (§ 2). Bishops are therefore strongly advised to stipulate that these norms be observed.

"From these prescriptions it follows that it is not even licit that the faithful use the formula of exorcism against Satan and the fallen angels, extracted from the one published by order of the Supreme Pontiff Leo XIII, and even less that they use the integral text of this exorcism. Bishops should take care to warn the faithful, if necessary, of this.

"Finally, for the same reasons, bishops are asked to be vigilant so that – even in cases that do not concern true demonic possession – those who are without the due faculty may not conduct meetings during which invocations, to obtain release, are uttered in which demons are questioned directly and their identity sought to be known.

"Drawing attention to these norms, however, should in no way distance the faithful from praying that, as Jesus taught us, they may be delivered from evil (cf. Mt 6:13). Finally, Pastors may take this opportunity to recall what the Tradition of the Church teaches concerning the role proper to the sacraments and the intercession of the Blessed Virgin Mary, of the Angels and Saints in the Christian's spiritual battle against evil spirits."

Cardinal Ratzinger
Prefect of the Congregation for the Doctrine of the Faith (1985).

PART FOUR

DELIVERING CITIES, TOWNS *&* LOCALITIES FROM

TERRITORIAL SPIRITS

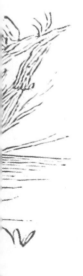

ΛULT

CHAPTER THIRTY

THE FESTAL SHOUT OF DELIVERANCE IN THE OLD & NEW TESTAMENTS

In 2017 the members of the New Springtime Community in Dublin were led to have a two-day festival entitled, "God Speaks to those who Praise Him". It was a wonderful occasion during which the Lord told us that we should go to a high place overlooking the city of Dublin to proclaim the festal shout of victory over evil spirits active in the city. Following a good deal of prayerful reflection and discussion we decided that on Saturday, August 19th we would go to Stella Maris retreat centre on the Hill of Howth, which overlooks the whole of Dublin. There we would spend two hours declaring in praise, that was loud and long, Christ's victory over the spiritual strongholds that oppress God's beloved people. We told members of other churches what we were intending to do and invited them to participate. On the appointed day 150 people from different places and churches participated in our festival of praise. Afterwards we received a lot of positive feedback about the event. We have also discovered since then that other groups in Ireland, Sicily and the Czech Republic were doing the same, having heard of the Dublin event. Here is an account of what the festal shout is, why it is important, and how to engage in it, in a liberating way.

In Biblical spirituality the prayer of appreciation is central. Among other things it is a matter of praising God, the giver of all good gifts. This reflection intends to focus on one particular form of praise known as the *teruah Yahweh,* i.e. the festal shout of victory. In the Old Testament there were frequent references to battles. Over and over again, the people of God had to contend with armies that were larger and better equipped than they were. But the Israelites had one great advantage. They had confidence that if they were following the Lord's will, God would be fighting with them. No matter what odds were stacked against them, they would be victorious. There are a number of examples of this. In Ex 14:14 there is a description of how the Jewish people were faced by the might of the Egyptian army. But Moses said to them, "Do not be afraid. Stand firm and you will see the deliverance the Lord will bring you today... The Lord will fight for you; you need only be still." In Ps 46:10, the Lord said in similar manner, "Be still, and know that I am God; I will be exalted among the nations, I will be exalted in the earth."

So it is not surprising to find that when the Jews marched into battle they would utter what the Bible refers to as the *teruah Yahweh.* It was a blood curdling war cry, which was simultaneously uttered by God and the heavenly hosts and by his soldiers on earth.

Speaking about the former Isa 42:11-13 says, "Let the people of Sela sing for joy; let them shout from the mountaintops. Let them give glory to the Lord and proclaim his praise in the coastlands. The Lord will march out like a champion, like a warrior he will stir up his zeal; with a shout he will raise the battle cry and will triumph over his enemies." Ps 24:8 adds, "Who is this King of glory? The Lord strong and mighty, the Lord mighty in battle."

In 2 Kings 6:13-23, we learn how king Aram sent a military force to Dothan to arrest the prophet Elisha. "When the servant of the man of God got up and went out early the next morning, an army with horses and chariots had surrounded the city. "Alas, my lord, what shall we do?" the servant asked. "Don't be afraid," the prophet answered. "Those who are with us are more than those who are with them." And Elisha prayed, "O Lord, open his eyes so he may see." Then the Lord opened the eyes of the servant's heart, and he looked and saw the hills full of horses and chariots of fire all around Elisha." Implicit in this text is the notion that God, the victorious king, is accompanied by the heavenly hosts. As Ps 91:11 promises, "God will command his angels concerning you to guard you in all your ways."

Jewish armies echoed the divine war cry as they went into

battle.[152] It was intended to strike terror into the hearts of their enemies. As a semi liturgical chant, it was also meant to express their unshakable confidence in the One who would give them the victory. As the Lord said in Zech 4:6-7, "You will succeed, not by military might or by your own strength, but by my spirit."

Arguably, in the Bible there are three forms of this kind of anticipatory praise, messianic, paschal and eschatological. The first has to do with the Old Testament when the Jews had intimations of the definitive victory of the messiah to come. The second has to do with the actual victory of Jesus over the enemies of humankind, Satan, sin, suffering and death. The third has to do with anticipating the final and definitive victory of God, which will be inaugurated by the second coming of Christ. We will look at each in turn.

---

152 Paul Hinnebusch, O.P., "The Battle Cry," in *Praise a Way of Life* (Ann Arbor: Word of Life, 1976), 12-14.

FREEDOM FROM EVIL SPIRITS

MESSIANIC PRAISE

The phrase, Messianic praise, refers to praise in the Old Testament that anticipated the liberating coming of Jesus the Messiah. There are many examples of this form of anticipatory praise. We will focus on a number of them in chronological order.

A] THE FALL OF JERICHO

When the Jews entered the promised land around 1,400 B.C. they came to Jericho, which was a few miles East of Jerusalem. Its population of about 1,200 was defended by double walls at the bottom and top of an earthen rampart. The outer wall was six feet thick and about 20–26 feet high. At the top of an earthen rampart was another big wall. The Israelites marched around the walls once every day for seven days with the priests and Ark of the Covenant. In Josh 6:5 we are told that the Lord said, "And when they make a long blast with the ram's horn, when you hear the sound of the trumpet, then all the people shall shout with a great shout, and the wall of the city will fall down flat." When the people did what the Lord had commanded, the walls of Jericho fell down. Archaeologists Garstang and Kenyon have found evidence that there was earthquake activity at the time the city met its end. If God used this means to accomplish the divine purposes, it was still a providential miracle, which happened at precisely the right moment. As Heb 11:30 says, "By faith the walls of Jericho fell, after the people had marched around them for seven days."

B] JONATHAN ATTACKS A GROUP OF PHILISTINES

Jonathan (c. 1000 BC) was the son of King Saul and a brother-in-law of David. In 1 Sam 13:19-22, we are told that the Jews were not allowed to have blacksmiths, "because the Philistines had said, 'Otherwise the Hebrews will make swords or spears'." However, we are told that Jonathan did have a sword. Without telling his father, King Saul, he decided that he would attack some Philistines at a place called Mishmash. However, he wanted to be sure that he was acting in the power of God, so "Jonathan said to his young armour-bearer, 'Come, let's go over to the outpost of those uncircumcised fellows. Perhaps the Lord will act in our behalf. Nothing can hinder the Lord from saving, whether by many or by few'." (1 Sam 14:6). This is a great statement of trust in the Lord. But Jonathan wanted to be sure that his intention to attack a much bigger force was within the will of God and not presumptuous on his part. We are told that, "Jonathan said, 'Come, then; we will cross over toward the men and let them see us. If they say to us, 'Wait there until we come to you', we will stay where we are and not go up to them. But if they say, 'Come up to us,' we will climb up, because that will be our sign that the Lord has given them into our hands'." (1 Sam 14:8-10) In the event the Philistines did taunt Jonathan, and said, "Come up to us and we'll teach you a lesson." (1 Sam 14:12) Then we are told what happened next, "So Jonathan said to his armour-bearer, 'Climb up after me; the Lord has given them into the hand of Israel'." (1 Sam 14:12) Within a short period of time Jonathan had killed 20 Philistines, while the remainder fled in panic. It is a typical Old Testament story which illustrates the point that when God is on the side of a courageous, faith-filled person who is seeking to do God's will, victory will be his or hers no matter how formidable the enemy might be. Although the sacred text makes no mention of the fact, we can assume that as Jonathan and his willing armour bearer attacked their enemies they were shouting the war cry which anticipated the victory, they knew in faith, that God would give them.

C] GIDEON AND THE THREE HUNDRED

In Judges 7 we are told how Gideon (c. 1191-1144 BC) had an army of 32,000 men. The Lord said, "Announce to the army, 'Anyone who trembles with fear may turn back and leave Mount Gilead'." So 22,000 men left, while 10,000 remained. The Lord still thought the army was too big, so he asked Gideon to urge the men to drink from a stream. "And the number of those who lapped, putting their hands to their mouths, was 300 men, but all the rest of the people knelt down to drink water. And the Lord said to Gideon, 'With the 300 men who lapped I will save you and give the Midianites into your hand, and let all the others go every man to his home'." (Jud 7:6-7) When the 300 reached the camp of the enemy Gideon said, "When I blow the trumpet, I and all who are with me, then blow the trumpets also on every side of all the camp and shout, 'For the Lord and for Gideon'."...Then the three companies blew the trumpets and broke the jars. They held in their left hands the torches, and in their right hands the trumpets to blow. And they cried out, 'A sword for the Lord and for Gideon!' Every man stood in his place around the camp, and all the army ran. They cried out and fled." (Jud 7:18; 20-21) It seems clear that although the Jewish army was very small, they attacked with a semi-liturgical battle cry of victory. It gave expression to their faith conviction that, despite their small numbers, the Lord would give them success. They did not shout in vain, thanks to the help of God they won. In Jud 7:22 we are told that, "When the three hundred trumpets sounded, the Lord caused the men throughout the camp to turn on each other with their swords."

D] THE VICTORY OF KING ABIJAH

In 2 Chron 13 there is another instructive example of the *teruwah Yahweh*. Around the year 912 BC there was a war between Abijah King of Judah and his father Jeroboam king of Israel. Apparently, there was a great battle when the army of Judah was outnumbered two to one. Nevertheless, King Abijah said to the Israelites, "We are observing the requirements of the Lord our God. But you have forsaken him [Jeroboam]. God is with us; he is our leader. His priests with their trumpets will sound the battle cry against you. Men of Israel, do not fight against the Lord, the God of your fathers, for you will not succeed." Things looked bad during the battle, because the army of Judah was being attacked from the front and the rear. We are told in 2 Chron 13:14-15, "Then they cried out to the Lord. The priests blew their trumpets and the men of Judah raised the battle cry. At the sound of their battle cry, God routed Jeroboam and all Israel before Abijah and Judah."

E] KING JEHOSHAPHAT'S VICTORY OVER THREE INVADING ARMIES

King Jehoshaphat reigned over Judah for 25 years from 870-849 BC. In 2 Chron 20 we are told that the king received news that his kingdom was about to be attacked by formidable armies. From a military point of view the position looked hopeless. Not surprisingly, the king was filled with fear and anxiety, but instead of wrestling with the problem; he nestled by faith in the Lord by means of prayer and fasting. Having poured out his heart to the Lord, Jehosophat waited for a divine response. It came through one of his priests who spoke a word of prophecy. "Your majesty," he said, "and all you people of Judah and Jerusalem, the Lord says you must not be discouraged or afraid to face this large army. The battle depends on God and not on you." (2 Chron 20:15)

We are told that: "early in the morning.... As the army set out, Jehoshaphat stood and said, 'Listen to me, Judah and people of Jerusalem! Have faith in the Lord your God and you will be upheld; have faith in his prophets and you will be successful'. After consulting the people, Jehoshaphat appointed men to sing to the Lord and to praise him for the splendor of his holiness as they went out at the head of the army, saying: 'Give thanks to the Lord, for his love endures forever'." In other words, the priests and musicians led the soldiers in shouting the *teruah Yahweh* as they marched into battle. The scriptures tell us what happened next, "As they began to sing and praise, the Lord set ambushes against the men of Ammon and Moab and Mount Seir who were invading Judah, and they were defeated." (2 Chron 20:20-22)

F] THE DEFEAT OF KING SENNACHERIB

Sennacherib was the King of Assyria from 705 to 681 BC. On one occasion he wrote to King Hezekiah, to say, "Surely you have heard what the kings of Assyria have done to all the countries, destroying them completely. And will you be delivered? Did the gods of the nations that were destroyed by my forefathers deliver them?" (2 Kings 19:11-12) He hoped that the Jewish king would capitulate. We are told that when he received the letter, Hezekiah "went up to the temple of the Lord and spread it out before the Lord. And Hezekiah prayed to the Lord: 'O Lord, God of Israel, enthroned between the cherubim, you alone are God over all the kingdoms of the earth. You have made heaven and earth. Give ear, O Lord, and hear; open your eyes, O Lord, and see; listen to the words Sennacherib has sent to insult the living God'." (2 Kings 19:14-16). A short time later the prophet Isaiah sent a reassuring message to the king, part of which said, "He [Sennacherib)]will not enter this city or shoot an arrow here. He will not come before it with shield or build a siege ramp against it. By the way that he came he will return; he will not enter this city, declares the Lord. I will defend this city and save it, for my sake and for the sake of David my servant." (2 Kings 19:32-34) Although in this instance we are not told whether the Jews expressed their confidence in God by means of the war cry of victory, we are informed about the outcome of their trust in God. "That night the angel of the Lord went out and put to death a hundred and eighty-five thousand men in the Assyrian camp. When the people got up the next morning — there were all the dead bodies! So Sennacherib King of Assyria broke camp and withdrew." (2 Kings 19:35-36) Some ancient historians like Josephus maintained that there was an outbreak of bubonic plague in the Assyrian army, which led to the death of most of its soldiers. In 681 BC King Sennacherib was assassinated by two of his sons.

G] THE VICTORY OF THE MACCABEES

In the second century BC the Maccabee brothers fought against those who disrupted their religious practices. They struggled against the Gentile king, Lysias who had gathered an army of 60,000 well-trained infantry and 5,000 cavalry. Judas Maccabeus's army came to meet them with only 10,000 men. When Judas saw how strong the enemy's army was, he prayed, "We will praise you, Saviour of Israel.

You broke the attack of the giant by the hand of your servant David and you let Saul's son Jonathan and the young man who carried his weapons defeat the entire Philistine army. Now in the same way let your people Israel defeat our enemy. Put them to shame, in spite of all their confidence in their infantry and cavalry. Make them afraid; let their bold strength melt away; let them tremble at the prospect of defeat. We love and worship you; so let us defeat our enemies, that we may then sing your praises." (1 Macc 4:20) Once again loud praise of God was the prelude to what was an unexpected Jewish victory from a human point of view.

CHAPTER THIRTY-TWO

THE WAR CRY EVOLVES INTO THE FESTAL SHOUT OF VICTORY

We find that when the chosen people had settled down in the Promised Land, they modified the battle cry for use in their temple worship.[153] It became the "festal shout" that is sometimes mentioned in the psalms. For example in Ps 33:1-3, we read, "Shout for joy in the Lord, O you righteous! Praise befits the upright. Give thanks to the Lord with the lyre; make melody to him with the harp of ten strings! Sing to him a new song; play skilfully on the strings, *with loud shouts* [my italics]." Again, in Ps 47:1-8 we read: "Clap your hands, all you nations; *shout to God* with cries of joy...God has ascended amid *shouts of joy*, the Lord amid the sounding of trumpets. Sing praises to God, sing praises; sing praises to our King, sing praises. For God is the King of all the earth; sing to him a psalm of praise." Ps 89:15 sums up this biblical attitude when it declares, "Blessed are the people who know the *festal shout*." There are a number of examples of the liberating power of the festal shout of victory in the Old and New Testaments.

Firstly, there is the case of the three young Jewish men, who, despite the threats of King Nebuchadnezzar, refused to worship false Gods. Although they were faced with the terrifying prospect of being thrown into a fiery furnace they proclaimed, "If we are thrown into the blazing furnace, the God we serve is able to save us from it, and he will rescue us from your hand, O king." It is worth noting that the commitment of the young men was unconditional. They knew that God could deliver them, but their faithfulness did not depend on being delivered. When they were thrown into the flames, instead of panicking, they expressed their unshakable faith by praising God.

---

153 Paul Hinnebusch, *Praise a Way of Life*, op. cit., 14-17.

It proved to be the prelude to their remarkable liberation. Suddenly, someone like a child of the gods was seen to be among them. The king was so impressed that he ordered that the three young men should be set free. When they emerged from the flames it was found that they had not been harmed.

Secondly, there is the curious case of the prophet Jonah. He experienced the trauma of being thrown into the sea and being swallowed by a whale. It must have been terrifying to be entombed in the dark, dank interior of this giant creature of the sea. Instead of being frozen with fear and despair, the prophet cried out his praises to the Lord. He said, "'When my life was ebbing away, I remembered you, Lord, and my prayer rose to you, to your holy temple. Those who cling to worthless idols forfeit the grace that could be theirs. But I, with a song of thanksgiving, will sacrifice to you. What I have vowed I will make good. Salvation comes from the Lord.' And the Lord commanded the fish, and it vomited Jonah onto dry land." (Jon 2:7-10) The praise of these heroes of faith in the Old Testament anticipated the coming of Jesus the Messiah and the liberating victory he would win for those who believed in him.

Thirdly, as a result of apostasy on the part of many Jews around 612 BC, God allowed them to be afflicted by military and natural disasters. The prophet Habakkuk had a sense that it was a matter of a happy fault, and that where sin abounded, God's grace would more abound. So in expectant faith he uttered his festal shout in anticipation of future blessing, "I will quietly wait for the day of trouble to come upon people who invade us. Though the fig tree should not blossom, nor fruit be on the vines, the produce of the olive fail and the fields yield no food, the flock be cut off from the fold and there be no herd in the stalls, yet I will rejoice in the Lord, I will take joy in the God of my salvation. God, the Lord, is my strength; he makes my feet like the deer's; he makes me tread on my high places." (Hab 3:16-19)

The festal shout as jubilation

In his interesting book *Sounds of Wonder*,[154] author Eddy Ensley indicated that as the gift of tongues declined in the early Church, it was sometimes augmented by what was referred to as jubilation. Jubilation occurs when such a great joy is conceived in the heart that it cannot be expressed in words, yet neither can it be concealed or hidden. It manifests itself with very happy gestures. The voice is excited to sing. In his commentary of Psalm 32 (33 in English versions), St Thomas Aquinas suggested that jubilation was the new song which Christians sing because of their renewal in grace: "That man truly sings in jubilation who sings about the good things of glory... the *jubilus* is an inexpressible joy which is not able to be expressed in words but even still the voice declares this vast expanse of joy... Moreover the things which are not able to be expressed, they are the good things of glory."[155] In his commentary on Psalm 46 (47 in English versions), Thomas wrote: "Jubilation is an unspeakable joy, which one cannot keep silent; yet neither can it be expressed. The reason that [this joy] cannot be expressed in words is that it is beyond comprehension.... Such is the goodness of God that it cannot be expressed, and even if it could be expressed, it could only imperfectly be expressed."[156] In her *Interior Castle*, St Teresa of Avila talked about the phenomenon when she wrote, "Our Lord sometimes causes in the soul a certain jubilation and a strange and mysterious kind of prayer. If He bestows this grace on you, praise Him fervently for it; I describe it so that you may know that it is something real. I believe that the faculties of the soul are closely united to God but that He leaves them at liberty to rejoice in their happiness together with the senses, although they do not know what they are enjoying nor how they do so. This may sound like nonsense but it really happens. So excessive is its jubilee that the soul will not enjoy it alone but speaks of it to all around so that they

---

154 (New York: Paulist Press, 1977).
155 In *Psalterium David*, Ps. 32:3 [33:3].
156 In *Psalterium David*, Ps. 46:1 [47:1].

may help it to praise God, which is its one desire."[157] There could be many reasons for jubilation, one of which is undoubtedly a certainty in the heart, that no matter what happens, God's victory over all negativity and evil will be declared. In the contemporary Church this form of confident joy is often expressed by singing spontaneously in lively tongues.

---

157   Chapter 6, par. 11.

CHAPTER THIRTY-THREE

PASCHAL *&* ESCHATOLOGICAL PRAISE

The expectancy foreshadowed in the Old Testament gave way to fulfilment in the life and ministry of Jesus Christ. There are at least two outstanding examples of the *teruah Yahweh* in the accounts of his passion and death on the cross.

The first occurred on Palm Sunday. The people greeted Jesus as the Messiah, as a political and military leader like King David of old, who would not only free them from the yoke of oppressive Roman rule but who would also enable the reign of God to reach to the whole world. So they waved palms, shouted raucous praises and chanted lines from Ps 118:25-27, "Hosanna; O Lord, grant us success. Blessed is he who comes in the name of the Lord. From the house of the Lord we bless you. The Lord is God, and he has made his light shine upon us. With boughs in hand, join in the festal procession up to the horns of the altar." I suspect that many people think that hosanna is a word of praise. Not so. In fact it literally means, "save us". But the Jews had such confidence that their prayer would be answered that it became a virtual cry of, "save us Lord, and we are confident that you will". When some disapproving Pharisees in the crowd said to Jesus, "Teacher, rebuke your disciples!", "I tell you," he replied, "if they keep quiet, the stones *will cry out*" (Luke 19:39-40). In other words, Jesus realised that the people's loud and enthusiastic shouts of praise were prophetic in a way they didn't consciously appreciate. Their *teruah*, their festal shout of victory was in fact anticipating the defeat, not of the Romans, but of Satan, by means of the saving death and resurrection of Jesus. As Col 2:15 declares, "And having disarmed the powers and authorities, he made a public spectacle of them, triumphing over them by the cross." Commenting on this verse, Pauline scholar James Dunne says that the imagery here, "is that of the public triumph, in which the defeated foes are led captive behind the triumphant general. The transformation of values, from the cross as the most shameful deaths, to the cross as a chariot leading the defeated powers in chains behind it, is about as audacious as one could imagine."

There is good reason to believe that Jesus also echoed the festal shout of the people on Palm Sunday, as he died on the cross. Betrayed, denied, and deserted, he even felt abandoned by God when he quoted a line from Ps 22:1, "My God, my God, why have you forsaken me?" Albert Gelin comments in his book *The Psalms are our Prayers*, "This complaint is not that of a rebel or of someone in despair. It is that of a just man, suffering but yet assured of the love and protection of the all holy God who will accompany him even to death... The cry is not, in the Jewish sense, an expression of despair, it does not express revolt, but remains in harmony with the devotion of the Old Testament and, in consequence, expresses a sense of communion with God."[158] Gelin also points out that if a Jew quoted the first line of a psalm, book or document, he was in virtue of that fact invoking it in its entirety. This would lead us to believe that Jesus silently recited the rest of Ps 22 in his mind. Having expressed his sense of anguish we have reason to believe that he strongly identified with the following words, "I will declare your name to my brothers; in the congregation I will praise you. You who fear the Lord, praise him! All you descendants of Jacob, honour him! Revere him, all you descendants of Israel!... From you comes the theme of my praise in the great assembly; before those who fear you will I fulfil my vows." (Ps 22:22-24) Jesus never lost trust in his Father's power to save him. As the end of his earthly life approached, he affirmed this truth. We are told that, "He *cried out in a loud voice*, Father into your hands I commend my spirit". (Lk 23:46) This was the *teruah* of Christ, his triumphant, festal cry of victory, which anticipated his glorious resurrection from the dead.

---

158   (Collegeville: Liturgical Press, 1964), 56.

Eschatological Praise

We are living in the last phase of human history. The power of Satan has been broken in principle by the death and resurrection of Jesus. As Paul wrote in Eph 1:19-20, "God raised him (Christ) from the dead and seated him on his right in the heavenly places, far above every ruler and authority and power and dominion and above every name that is named not only in this age but in the age to come." Knowing this to be true he asked in 1 Cor 15:55-57, "Where, O death, is your victory? Where, O death, is your sting... thanks be to God! He gives us the victory through our Lord Jesus Christ." Satan will be finally defeated in practice when Christ returns in glory. No wonder the commonest cry of the early Church was *maranatha*, i.e. "Come Lord Jesus" (Rev 22:20). Like the cry of hosanna, it was a prayer of petition, which was uttered with such expectant faith that it was transformed into a festal shout of praise. This festal shout of the first Christians anticipated the final and definitive victory of God over the powers of darkness, in human history.

Writing about the second coming of Jesus, St Paul wrote in I Tim 3:1-5, "But mark this: There will be terrible times in the last days. People will be lovers of themselves, lovers of money, boastful, proud, abusive, disobedient to their parents, ungrateful, unholy, without love, unforgiving, slanderous, without self-control, brutal, not lovers of the good, treacherous, rash, conceited, lovers of pleasure rather than lovers of God - having a form of godliness but denying its power." In 1 Thess 4:16-17, Paul added, "the Lord himself will come down from heaven, *with a loud command*, with the voice of the archangel and with the trumpet call of God, and the dead in Christ will rise first. After that, we who are still alive and are left will be caught up together with them in the clouds to meet the Lord in the air. And so we will be with the Lord forever." Just as the *teruah* of Jesus on the cross inaugurated a final victory over Satan, so his great *teruah* at the end of time will consummate that victory in a definitive way.

CHAPTER THIRTY-FOUR

ANTICIPATORY THANKSGIVING

At this point we will look at a form of prayer that is closely related to the festal shout of victory. Reading St Paul, especially Romans chapter one, it is evident that he saw thankful appreciation as an act of fundamental religious importance. The word to "thank" in English is taken from the Old English meaning, "to think". Appreciation as thanksgiving means that one is mindful and grateful for the natural and supernatural gifts of God. St Paul not only thanked God repeatedly himself, he said to people of faith, "pray continually; give thanks in *all circumstances*, for this is God's will for you in Christ Jesus," (1 Thes 5:17-18) and in Eph 5:20 he added, "always give thanks to God the Father *for everything*, in the name of our Lord Jesus Christ". It is clear that we should thank God for the graces and blessings of life. It is good not to take them for granted, but rather to call them to mind with gratitude. But apparently St Paul implies that we should also thank God for the bad things, like illness and personal sin, as forms of postponed success. No wonder Paul said that it is God's will that we do so.

How can we thank God for the misfortunes and sins in our lives? It is not that we thank God for these evils in themselves, but because we believe that they have been embraced by divine providence. Over the years I have come to realise that no matter what misfortunes I endure or what mistakes I make, they are integrated into God's saving plan for my life. So I firmly believe that, strange as it may seem, sin and suffering can become the birthplace of blessing. Evil does not have the final say. That word belongs to God and it is a redeeming word of blessing and victory.

There is an outstanding biblical example of what I mean. In the book of Genesis we are told that, because of the envy of his brothers,

Joseph was sold into slavery in Egypt. When the Pharaoh had disturbing dreams that none of his counsellors could interpret, Joseph interpreted his dreams, predicting seven years of plentiful food, followed by seven years of famine. To Joseph's surprise, the Pharaoh appointed him as minister of food. Under Joseph's care, many supplies were stored and the land prospered. When famine struck, people from all the surrounding lands came to buy food from him. The famine also struck Canaan, and Joseph's brothers eventually came to Egypt to buy grain. When they met Joseph he recognised them, but they failed to recognise him. Finally, overcome with emotion Joseph revealed himself to his brothers. He said to them, "I am Joseph! Is my father still living?" But his brothers were not able to answer him, because they were terrified at his presence. Then Joseph said to his brothers, "Come close to me." When they had done so, he said, "I am your brother Joseph, the one you sold into Egypt! And now, do not be distressed and do not be angry with yourselves for selling me here, because *it was to save lives that God sent me ahead of you...* to preserve for you a remnant on earth and to save your lives by a great deliverance. "So then, it was not you who sent me here, but God." (Gen 45:2-8)

Joseph's statement is a remarkable one when you think about it. God used the heartless treachery of his brothers as the providential source of *their* future blessing. There is an intimation in this story of the way in which Jesus our brother would be delivered into the hands of the chief priests and the Roman authorities who would cruelly murder him. And just as Joseph's suffering became a source of blessing for those who inflicted it, so Jesus' suffering and death became the source of salvation and healing for those who had inflicted it by their sins. As we declare in the Easter liturgy, "O happy fault, O necessary sin of Adam which gained for us so great a Redeemer!" St Paul echoed that sentiment when he wrote, God has made us "prisoners of disobedience in order that God might show mercy" (Rm 11:32), and "Where sin abounded, the grace of God more abounded" (Rm 5:21).

Surely this principle can be extended not only to our sins, but also to our sufferings and the evils we face. We can thank God *in all* circumstances, rather than *for all* circumstances, in the knowledge that they can become the springboards to God's grace either sooner or later. I can remember an occasion that occurred many years ago. I was due to attend a conference for priests. I travelled to it by motorbike. As I went along the road I was singing hymns. At one point I prayed; "Lord if you have any message for the conference please speak to me." Then I felt inwardly that the Lord was saying, "tell your fellow priests about the pearl of great price." While I was glad to get that word, I didn't really know what it meant. When I got to the conference there was a preparatory prayer session. During a quiet time the image of an oyster came to mind. It was on the mud of the sea floor surrounded by water. I understood that the sea floor was the world, the sea the Spirit, and the oyster, the human person. Then I felt that the Lord was saying, "Think of how a pearl is formed. Grit and dirt get from the sea-bed into the oyster. It cannot expel it. So it secretes a milky liquid which surrounds the grit over a seven-year period. The greater the irritation the greater the pearl that is finally formed. It is the same with the human heart. The sin of the world makes an entry. But in my compassion, I weave the pearl of mercy around it. The greater the sin the greater the pearl that is finally formed. Tell the priests not to be disheartened by their weaknesses. I will bring good from evil, blessing from failure."

In Phil 4:6 St Paul said, "Do not be anxious about anything, but in every situation, by prayer and petition, *with thanksgiving*, present your requests to God." When we Christians are confronted by the powers of evil, there is no need to be anxious or afraid. Trusting in God, we can be confident, no matter what failures we experienced in the past, that we will receive whatever graces and blessings we need in order to carry out the will of God. As Paul said, these requests should be offered to God in a spirit of anticipatory thanksgiving, St John assured us, "This is the confidence we have in approaching God: that if we ask anything according to his will, he hears us. And if we know that he hears us - whatever we ask - *we know that we have what we asked of him*" (1 Jn 5:14-15). So this kind of thanksgiving is closely related to the festal shout of praise. Both anticipate the victory the Lord gives to those who trust in him.

Surely, St Joan of Arc epitomised this kind of faith. At the age of sixteen she had been directed by God to lead the French army and to have Charles, the dauphin, crowned as rightful king of France. She was able to confirm the divine origin of her prophecy by words of knowledge. For example, although she had never met Charles the Dauphin, she recognised him in his court when he was dressed in a disguise. However, the irrefutable sign or proof of Joan's authenticity was the French army's miraculous victory over the English at Orleans on May 8ᵗʰ 1429. Having foretold that her mission would last "one year, scarcely more," she went on to other victories, and managed to have the dauphin properly anointed at Reims on July 17ᵗʰ 1429.[159] In our struggle against the forces of evil, like St Joan, we need invincible confidence that God will give us the victory, a confidence that is best expressed in anticipatory praise and thanksgiving. As 1 Jn 4:4 assures us, "the one who is in you is greater than the one who is in the world."

---

159 Cf. "The Mission of Joan of Arc" in *Medieval Hagiography: An Anthology,* ed., Thomas Head (New York: Routledge, 2001), 805-834.

CHAPTER THIRTY-FIVE

THE FESTAL SHOUT & SPIRITUAL WARFARE TODAY

When he was still a cardinal in 1976, John Paul II spoke these prophetic words in Philadelphia, "We are now standing in the face of the greatest historical confrontation humanity has ever experienced. I do not think that the Christian Community realise this fully. We are now facing the final confrontation between the Church and the anti-church, between the Gospel and the anti-gospel, between Christ and the anti-Christ. The confrontation lies within the plans of Divine Providence. It is, therefore, in God's Plan, and it must be a trial which the Church must take up, and face courageously."

We are currently witnessing apostasy on an unprecedented scale in Europe, including Britain and Ireland. Millions of people are turning their backs on the Church and living as if God does not exist. One is reminded of the words of the Lord in Jer 2:13, "My people have committed two sins: They have forsaken me, the spring of living water, and have dug their own cisterns, broken cisterns that cannot hold water." The last verse of the book of Judges says, "In those days Israel had no king; everyone did as they saw fit." Nowadays it could be adapted to read, "In our days Britain and Ireland acknowledge no ultimate authority and the citizens do whatever they think is permissible themselves."

According to the Bible, spiritual challenges like these are influenced by the devil. Jesus referred to the evil as "the ruler of the world" in Jn 12:31, and as, "the prince of this word" in Jn 14:30. In 1 Jn 5:19 we are told that, "the whole world is under the control of the evil one."

On one occasion Jesus answered the all important question, why is it that so many do not accept the Gospel? He did so by telling the parable of the sower. He said, "When anyone hears the message about the kingdom and *does not understand it*, the evil one comes and snatches away what was sown in their heart. This is the seed sown along the path." (Mt 13:19)

Although most people know about Jesus and have heard his word, in one way or another, they neither understand or believe. Speaking about them, St Paul observed, "The god of this age [i.e. Satan] has blinded the minds of unbelievers so that they cannot see the light of the Gospel." (2 Cor 4:4)

However, Paul went on to say in 2 Cor 10:3-5 that, "For though we walk in the flesh, we are not waging war according to the flesh. For the weapons of our warfare are not of the flesh but have divine power to destroy strongholds [i.e. of Satan in the mind and heart]. We destroy arguments and every lofty opinion raised against the knowledge of God, and take every thought captive to obey Christ." So according to Paul we are involved in spiritual warfare against a formidable enemy. The festal shout not only overcomes the powers of evil, at the same time it calls down the anointing of the Lord on those who praise him. In 2 Chron 5:13-14 we read about a remarkable example of this grace, "The trumpeters and singers joined in unison, as with one voice, to give praise and thanks to the Lord. Accompanied by trumpets, cymbals and other instruments, they raised their voices in praise to the Lord and sang: "He is good; his love endures forever." Then the temple of the Lord was filled with a cloud, and the priests could not perform their service because of the cloud, for the glory of the Lord filled the temple of God." Where God's *shekhinah* glory is present, the evil spirits withdraw into the shadows.

HISTORICAL EXAMPLES

Some charismatic and Pentecostal scholars believe that evil spirits can oppress cities, towns and localities. For instance, in Dan 10:13 we learn that, "the prince of the Persian kingdom resisted me 21 days. Then Michael, one of the chief princes, came to help me." It is thought that Daniel was describing how he had to contend, for a time, with an evil territorial spirit that was eventually overcome by the archangel Michael, the guardian of the Jewish people.

In chapter six of *The Life of St Francis of Assisi* by St Bonaventure, there seems to be a clear reference to these oppressive spirits. "It befell once that he came unto Arezzo at a time when the whole city was shaken by a civil war that threatened its speedy ruin. As he was lodging in the outskirts of the city, he beheld the demons exulting above it, and inflaming the angry citizens to mutual slaughter. Then, that he might put to flight those powers of the air that were stirring up the strife, he sent forward as his herald Brother Silvester, a man of dovelike simplicity, saying: "Go out before the city gate, and, on behalf of God Almighty, command the demons in the power of obedience to depart with all speed." The Brother, in true obedience, hastened to perform his Father's behests, and, coming before the presence of the Lord with thanksgiving, began to cry with a loud voice before the city gate: "On behalf of God Almighty,... depart far from here, all you demons!"[160] At once the city was restored to a state of peace.

Peter Wagner, of Fuller Theological Seminary with campuses in California, Arizona, Washington, Colorado, and Texas, has written about territorial spirits in a book entitled, *Wrestling with Dark Angels: Toward a Deeper Understanding of the Supernatural Forces in Spiritual Warfare*. He wrote, "Satan delegates high ranking members of the hierarchy of evil spirits to control nations, regions, tribes, peoples, groups, neighbourhoods and other significant social networks of human beings throughout the world. Their major assignment is to prevent God from being glorified in their territory, which they do through directing the activity of lower ranking demons."[161] Although some aspects of his approach have proven to be controversial, e.g. the notion of "spiritual mapping", that quotation seems to be broadly in line with the understanding of St Francis of Assisi.

---

160 St Bonaventure, *The Life of St Francis of Assisi* (Charlotte: Tan Classics, 2010), chapter VI.
161 (Raleigh: Regal Books, 1990), 77.

Guidelines for the festal shout of deliverance

In the course of a two-day festival of praise in Dublin, in May 2017, there was a prophetic word in which God asked those present to join with sisters and brothers from other churches to proclaim God's victory over the powers of evil. When we prayed about this prophecy, we felt that it was a call to proclaim God's triumph over the strongholds of evil that influence Irish and British people. In Joel 2:1 we are told that in such circumstances of danger the believers should declare God's victory over the city, town or locality. "Blow a trumpet in Zion; sound an alarm on my holy mountain! Let all the inhabitants of the land tremble, for the day of the Lord is coming; it is near."

As a result, many men and women from the Christian churches intended to hold praise gatherings on high ground overlooking the places where they live and evangelise in order to utter the festal shout of victory over the spirits of evil which oppress our people. Rather than being intercessory, this form of prayer is mainly declaratory, praising God's greatness, while affirming Christ's victory over the powers of darkness. Just as Jesus formed a whip and drove the buyers and sellers out of the temple in Jerusalem, so the risen Jesus lashes out at the evil spirits with the whip of his righteous zeal and indignation while shouting, "Get out of here! Get out of this city/town/locality." We the believers, join with him in saying the same thing by means of the festal shout of victory. Here are five points connected with this kind of praise.

Firstly, before the appointed day when God's victory over evil spirits is declared by means of the festal shout the participants could prepare by means of mourning and prudent fasting (or alternative acts of self-denial). Jesus said in his beatitudes, "Blessed are those who mourn, for they will be comforted" (Mt 5:4). What our Lord had in mind here was mourning for personal and corporate sin. We need to mourn for the many ways in which people, and especially those of our own locality, have turned their backs on the person and the law of the Lord. In Joel 2:12 the notion of mourning for sin was associated with fasting. It said, "Yet even now," declares the Lord, "return to me with all your heart, with fasting, with weeping, and with mourning." In Dan 10:2-3, we are told that in such a situation, "I, Daniel, mourned for three weeks. I ate no choice food; no meat or wine touched my lips." Therefore, in a permissive age of self-indulgence, such as ours, Christians would do well to engage in moderate fasting as a means of making reparation for sin and preparing for the festal shout.

Secondly, when the day of the festal shout of victory arrives, it is uttered with expectant faith. It is a matter of believing that what we desire, i.e. deliverance from evil spirits, is within the centrality of God's will. That is why Jesus taught us to pray, "deliver us from the evil one." (Mt 6:13) As 1 Jn 5:14 assures us, "And this is the confidence that we have toward him, that if we ask anything according to his will he hears us. And if we know that he hears us in whatever we ask, we know that we have the requests that we have asked of him." Notice that the inspired author does not say we will get what we desire, rather he asserts that we are receiving it.

Thirdly, whether praise is expressed in our native language or in tongues, it should be loud, long and accompanied, if needs be, by such things as the shaking of tambourines, the banging of drums and bodhrans (Irish hand drums), the clanging of cymbals, blowing of whistles and the clapping of hands. These can be accompanied by the waving of flags and dancing. As Ps 150:3-5 says, "Praise him with the sounding of the trumpet, praise him with the harp and lyre, praise him with tambourine and dancing, praise him with the strings and flute, praise him with the clash of cymbals." The author of Sir 43:29-33 adds, "Where shall we find the strength to praise him? For he is great-er than all his works. Terrible is the Lord and very great, and mar-vellous is his power. When you praise the Lord, exalt him as much as you can; for he will surpass even that. When you exalt him, put forth all your strength, and do not grow weary, for you cannot praise him enough. Who has seen him and can describe him? Or who can praise him as he is?"

Fourthly, praises can have a prophetic dimension. Those who are praising God are open to hear God's revealed word. In Dan 2:20-22 we read, "God is wise and powerful! Praise him forever and ever. He controls the times and the seasons; he makes and unmakes kings; it is he who gives wisdom and understanding. He reveals things that are deep and secret", which are in accord with the word and will of God. God's revelation can come in many ways, e.g. by highlighting what spirits to pray against, by means of a relevant scripture text, a meaningful image, vision, mental message, word of knowledge or prophetic words.

Fifthly, in Matt 12:43-45 Jesus warned, "When the unclean spirit has gone out of a person, it passes through waterless places seeking rest, but finds none. Then it says, 'I will return to my house from which I came.' And when it comes, it finds the house empty, swept and put in order. Then it goes and brings with it seven other spirits more evil than itself, and they enter and dwell there, and the last state of that person is worse than the first." So when we command the evil spirits to depart from a place, we also call down God's transforming Holy Spirit asking for the grace of peace and revival. With Ps 80:18-19 we can pray, "revive us, and we will call on your name. Restore us, O Lord God Almighty; make your face shine upon us, that we may be saved."

CONCLUSION

My personal conviction about the importance of enthusiastic thanksgiving and praise of this kind was nurtured during the Troubles in Northern Ireland. Because ecumenically minded Christians seemed to face impossible odds we had to rely solely on God. For example, an inter-faith conference was held in Belfast during the general strike of 1974. There was the threat of violence in the streets and of power failures. Nevertheless, over a thousand Protestants and Catholics gathered in Church House in the centre of the city for a 'Festival of Praise'. It was a remarkable experience. There was an outburst of strong, sustained praise such as I had never heard before. God's anointing fell upon us and we were graced with the festal shout, the kind that anticipates the liberating action of God. In a prophecy the Lord called upon us to be united as his army. "The work and the weapons are one," God said, "they are praise." At that time we had an intimation of the peace that would come to Northern Ireland many years later as a result of the Good Friday agreement.

While one can often see the positive effects of the festal shout when we affirm God's victory over the powers of darkness in our lives, such as physical and mental illness, addictions, and spiritual oppression, it requires a great deal of faith to believe that cities are being delivered from evil influences even though there may be no discernible effects. But we can take refuge in what we read in Lk 10:17-19, "The seventy-two returned with joy and said, 'Lord, even the demons submit to us in your name.' He replied, 'I saw Satan fall like lightning from heaven. I have given you authority to trample on snakes and scorpions and to overcome all the power of the enemy; nothing will harm you'." Having praised God on high ground, we descend to the lower places where people live, in order to proclaim the Gospel of salvation with conviction and effectiveness.

CHAPTER THIRTY-SIX

SUGGESTED GUIDELINES FOR EVENT ORGANISERS

1. One person takes a leadership role. He or she begins by explaining what the festal shout of victory is about while inviting believers in Jesus - Catholics, Protestants, Pentecostals, Orthodox, and Messianic Jews - to join him or her in a festal shout of victory event.

2. Those volunteers form an organising committee, ideally with representative members from the Christian churches.

3. Choose a gathering place in the outdoors, ideally on an elevated piece of ground overlooking the city or town. It should not be in a place where the believers would interfere with the activities of the general public. You might have to get permission to do this from the landowner and/or the police. You might also need insurance cover.

4. Choose a date when people would be free to attend.

5. Advertise the praise event e.g.
   • Contact people who would be interested by means of the social media.
   • Try to have one of the leaders interviewed on local radio about the event.
   • Put an ad about it in the local paper and in parish newsletters.

6. Encourage the people to bring such things as
   • Musical instruments, e.g. tambourines, drums, bodhrans (i.e. hand drums), whistles, a Jewish Shofar etc.
   • Flags of different kinds.
   • Bibles and hymn books

7. Invite a music group/s to help in leading the praise. Remember there may be no electrical means of amplification. The

musicians need to have a spiritual understanding of the festal shout of victory and supplied with suitable hymns for
the occasion, e.g. Lift high the banners of love; There are
the days of Elijah; He is Lord; Shine Jesus Shine; Jesus name
above all Names etc.

8. Have an explanatory, hortatory input about the festal shout.
The above notes could be used. They can be purchased from
the New Springtime Community (See community website).
A loud hailer will be needed.

9. The length of the praise event should be between an hour
and two hours.

10. A picnic could follow or precede the praise which encourages fellowship.

Suggested Order of a Festal Shout Event

A] Welcome everyone

Then go on to explain the thinking behind the event.

B] Affirm the unity of those present

There is a need to begin by repenting of sins against unity both in
and between the churches by turning away from those attitudes and
actions that disrupt union of mind and heart. In Phil 2:1-5 we read,
"If you have any encouragement from being united with Christ, if
any comfort from his love, if any fellowship with the Spirit, if any
tenderness and compassion, then make my joy complete by being
like-minded, having the same love, being one in spirit and purpose.
Do nothing out of selfish ambition or vain conceit, but in humility consider others better than yourselves. Each of you should look
not only to your own interests, but also to the interests of others.
Your attitude should be the same as that of Christ Jesus." Did we as
Catholics or Protestants consider others to be inferior to ourselves,
did we put our own interests ahead of those of members of other
groups or churches? Let us ask God to forgive our offences against
loving unity. Have everyone give the sign of peace by saying, "Peace

be with you, we are one in Christ." An appropriate hymn could be sung, e.g. "Bind us together."

C] PRAISE GOD

Led by the music group, those who have gathered spend time in prayer and praise, remembering that Ps 100:4 says, "Enter his gates with thanksgiving and his courts with praise; give thanks to him and praise his name." Encourage worship that is loud and long.

D] THE FESTAL SHOUT

There is a reference to the festal shout of victory in Zech 3:14-16 were the prophet says, "Shout for joy, O daughter Zion! Sing joyfully, O Israel! Be glad and exult with all your heart . . . , The Lord has . . . has turned away your enemies; the King of Israel, the Lord, is in your midst." Notice the succession of imperatives, shout, sing joyfully, exult gradly. The festal shout of victory affirms the fact that Jesus is tearing down the strongholds of Satan. When we express the festal shout of victory, we are affirming God's victory over spirits such as those of apostasy, rebellion, pride, idolatry, addiction and impurity. As we do so Jesus wields the whip of his righteous anger and drives them out of God's dwelling place (cf. Jn 2:13-22). We express it in loud hymns. Whether praise is expressed in our native language or in tongues, it should be enthusiastic. Those who are praising God are encouraged to hear and to hare God's revealed word. Those who are present can be invited to share any word of revelation they have received by means of a relevant scripture text, a meaningful image, vision, mental message, word of knowledge or prophetic word utterance.

CONCLUSION

I have spoken about the nature and practice of the festal shout of victory on a number of occasions, not only in Ireland but in a number of other countries. On each occasion the teaching has been greeted with enthusiasm, and subsequently I have heard of a number of festal shouts which have been organised in high places here in Ireland and as far away as Palermo in Sicily, Bologna in Italy and Zeliv in the Czech Republic. The following slightly modified extract from the Breastplate of St Patrick, also known as The Lorica of Saint Patrick, would be appropriate on such occasions because it is so mindful of the power of God and the heavenly hosts.

"As we utter the festal shout of victory we summon today
All the powers between us and those evils,
Against every cruel and merciless power
that may oppose our bodies and souls,
Against incantations of false prophets,
Against black laws of pagans,
Against false laws of heretics,
Against craft of idolatry,
Against spells of witches and and wizards,
Against every knowledge that corrupts people's bodies and souls;
Christ shield us today
Against poison, against burning,
Against drowning, against wounding,
So that there may come to us an abundance of reward. Amen."

SOME HELPFUL BOOKS & WEBSITES

PART ONE

Collins, Pat. "Faith and Protection From anxiety" in *Finding Faith in Troubled Times* (Dublin: Columba, 1993), pp. 52-101.

Collins, Pat. *Reducing Stress and Finding Peace* (Dublin: Veritas, 2002).

Ensley, Eddie. *Prayer that Relieves Stress & Worry* (Fortson, GA: Contemplative Press, 2007).

Tillich Paul. *The Courage to Be* (Fontana: London, 1962).

Lonergan, Bernard, "Feelings" in *Method in Theology* (London: Darton, Longman & Todd, 1972), 30-4.

Rowe, Dorothy. *Beyond Fear* (London: Harper/Collins, 2007).

von Balthasar, Hans Urs. *The Christian and Anxiety* (San Francisco: Ignatius, 2000).

PART TWO

www.alcoholicsanonymous.ie

www.alcoholics-anonymous.org.uk

www.gamblersanonymous.ie

www.gamblersanonymous.org.uk

www.na-ireland.org

ukna.org/contacts

www.overeatersanonymous.ie

www.oagb.org.uk

www.recovery.org/...the-neurotics-anonymous-12-step-recovery-program

https://minnesotarecovery.org/.../sexaholics-anonymous-international

www.al-anon-ireland.org

www.al-anonuk.org.uk

www.helpself.com/directory/codependency.htm

https://cametobelieve.org/about_us

I have found that the following publications are particularly helpful.

Anderson, Neil. *Freedom from Addiction: Breaking the Bondage of Addiction and Finding Freedom in Christ* (Minneapolis: Bethany House, 1996).

Beattie, Melody. *Co-dependent No More: How to Stop Controlling Others and Start Caring for Yourself* (Minnesota: Hazelden, 1992).

May, Gerald. *Addiction and Grace: Love and Spirituality in the Healing of Addictions* (New York: Harper & Row, 1989).

Linn, Dennis & Matthew and Sheila Fabricant. *Belonging: Bonds of Healing and Recovery* (New York: Paulist, 1991).

Spiegelman, Erica. *Rewired: A Bold New Approach To Addiction and Recover* (New York: Hatherleigh, 2015).

Snyder, Clarence et Al. *Our A.A. Legacy to the Faith Community: A Twelve-Step Guide for Those Who Want To Believe.* (Winter Park, FL: Came to Believe Publications, 2005).

Wilson, Bill & Aaron Cohen. *The Big Book of Alcoholics Anonymous*

Including 12 Steps, Guides & Prayers (CreateSpace Independent Publishing Platform, 2015).

PART THREE

1] RELEVANT CHURCH TEACHING

This is a short list of important Church references to the deliverance ministry.

- In 1975, the Congregation for the Doctrine of the Faith published *Christian Faith and Demonology.*
- In 1983, the new *Code of Canon Law* was published. Canon, 1172 is about the appointment of exorcists.

- In 1985, Cardinal Ratzinger, the Prefect of the Congregation for the Doctrine of the Faith, published a short document entitled, *Letter to Ordinaries Regarding Norms of Exorcism.*
- Par. 1673 of the *Catechism of the Catholic Church*, is about exorcism.
- The Church's official Rite *Of Exorcism and Certain Supplications* was published in 1999. An official English translation was approved for publication in 2017 and is available to priests who have the approval of their local ordinaries from the publishing house of the American Bishops Conference.

2] SOME HELPFUL WRITINGS ON DELIVERANCE MINISTRY

Amorth, Gabriele. *An Exorcist Tells His Story.* (San Francisco: Ignatius, 1999).

Amorth, Gabriele. *An Exorcist: More Stories.* (San Francisco: Ignatius, 2002).

Blai, Adam C. *Possession, Exorcism, & Hauntings.* (GB: Amazon, 2014).

Clark, Randy. *The Biblical Guidebook to Deliverance.* (Lake Mary, Florida: Charisma House, 2015).

Congregation for Divine Worship and the Discipline of the Sacraments. *Exorcisms and Certain Supplications.* (Washington: USCBC, 2017).

Collins, Pat. *Unveiling the Heart: How to overcome Evil in the Christian Life* (Dublin: Veritas, 1995).

Collins, Pat. "Exorcism and the Falling Phenomenon" *Maturing in the Spirit* (Dublin: Columba, 1991), 141-156.

Collins, Pat. "Faith and Deliverance from Evil" *Finding Faith in Troubled Times* (Dublin: Columba, 1993), 102-147.

Collins, Pat. "Spiritual Warfare" *Spirituality for the 21st Century* (Dublin: Columba, 1999), 170-179.

Collins, Pat. "Atheism and the Father of Lies" *The Broken Image* (Dublin: Columba, 2002), 208- 220.

Collins, Pat. "Mother Teresa's Dark Night of the Soul" *Doctrine and Life* (Nov. 2001), 562-566.

Collins, Pat. "Spirit Forces" in Dara de Faoite, *Paranormal Ireland* (Ashbourne: Maverick House, 2002), 67-84.

Collins, Pat. "The Ministry of Deliverance" *He Has Anointed Me* Luton: New Life Publishing, 2005), 53-64.

Collins, Pat. "The Paranormal and Spirituality" *Mind and Spirit: Spirituality and Psychology in Dialogue* (Dublin: Columba, 2006), 113-128.

Collins, Pat. "St Patrick's Nightmare," in *The Broken Image* (Dublin: Columba, 2002), 100-104.

Doctrinal Commission of ICCRS. *Deliverance Ministry.* (Vatican City: ICCRS, 2017).

Driscoll, Mike. *Demons, Deliverance & Discernment.* (El Cajon, Calif: Catholic Answers, 2015).

House of Healing. *Deliverance Ministry.* (The Netherlands: House of Healing Den Bosch, 2017).

Lendrum, William H. *Confronting the Paranormal: A Christian Perspective.* (Belfast: Lendrum, 2002).

Leyshon, Dr Gareth. "Exorcism and Prayers for Deliverance: The Position of the Catholic Church. A Historical Review of Developments since the late 19th Century and a Summary of the Norms now Applicable." http://www.drgareth.info/Deliverance-X.pdf

Linn, Denis & Matthew. *Deliverance Prayer: Experiential, Psychological and Theological Approaches.* (New York: Paulest Press, 1981).

Lloyd-Jones, Martyn, *The Christian Warfare: An Exposition of Eph 6:10-13* (Grand Rapids: Baker, 1976).

Lozano, Neal. *Unbound: A Practical Guide to Deliverance.* (Grand Rapids, Michigan: Chosen, 2003).

Lozano, Neal. *Resisting the Devil: A Catholic Perspective on Deliverance.* (Huntington IN: Our Sunday Visitor, 2010).

Mac Nutt, Francis. *Deliverance From Evil Spirits: A Practical Manual.* (Grand Rapids: Chosen Books, 2009).

Porteous, Bishop Julian. *Manual of Minor Exorcisms: For the use of Priests* (London: Catholic Truth Society, 2012).

Scanlon, Michael & Cirner, Randall J. *Deliverance From Evil Spirits: A Weapon for Spiritual Warfare.* (Ann Arbor, Michigan: Servant Books, 1980).

Stayne, Damian. "Liberation from Evil Spirits," in *Renew Your Wonders: Spiritual gifts for Today* (Luton: New Life, 2017), pp. 233-279.

Suenens, Cardinal Joseph. *Renewal & the Powers of Darkness.* (London: Darton, Longman & Todd, 1983).

Wagner, Doris. *How To Cast out Demons: A Guide to the Basics.* Minneapolis: Chosen, 2000).

3] THESE ARE SOME USEFUL WEBSITES.

https://ministryteamtools3.blogspot.com/

www.heartofthefather.com

PART FOUR

Collins, Pat. "Courageous Faith Expressed in Praise," in *Finding Faith in Troubled Times* (Dublin: Columba, 1993), pp. 95-100.

Ensley, Eddie. *Sounds of Wonder: Speaking in Tongues in the Catholic Tradition* (New York: Paulist Press, 1977).

Hammond, Frank. *Praise - A Weapon of Warfare and Deliverance* (Kirkwood MO: Impact Christian Books, 2015).

Hinnebusch, Paul. *Praise a Way of Life* (Ann Arbor, Mich: Word of Life, 1976)

Vadia, Maria. *Jesus Man of War: His Victory For Those Who Praise Him* (Golets, CA: Queenship Company, 2015).